# AT THE FOOT OF THE MOUNTAIN

## Discovering Images For Emotional Healing

Alla Renée Bozarth, Ph.D.

CompCare® Publishers

Minneapolis, Minnesota

Bozarth, Alla Renee, 1947-
    At the foot of the mountain: discovering images for emotional healing/by Alla
Renee Bozarth.
        p.    cm.
ISBN 0-89638-224-9
1. Spiritual healing. 2. Imagination—Religious aspects—Christianity. 3. Consola-
tion. 4. Spiritual life—Anglican authors. 5. Bozarth, Alla Renee, 1947-    . I. Title.
BT732.5.B69 1990                                                          90-38179
248.8'6—dc20                                                               CIP

Cover and interior illustrations by Toshi Maeda.

Cover and interior design by MacLean and Tuminelly

Inquiries, orders, and catalog requests should be addressed to:
CompCare Publishers
2415 Annapolis Lane
Minneapolis, Minnesota 55441
Call toll free 800/328-3330
(Minnesota residents 612/559-4800)

| 6 | 5 | 4 | 3 | 2 | 1 |
|---|---|---|---|---|---|
| 95 | 94 | 93 | 92 | 91 | 90 |

To the angels in our lives—those messengers
from God who help us to live honestly
and to the full.

# Contents

Sheed and Ward
*Love's Prism: Reflections from
the Heart of a Woman*

North Star Press
*Stars in Your Bones:
Emerging Signposts on Our
Spiritual Journeys*

*Audio Tapes by Alla Renée Bozarth*

CompCare Publishers
*Life is Goodbye/Life is Hello*

*Dance for Me When I Die*

*Before the Beginning and after the End . . .*

This book catches me on the wing.

It is a book of Between. So it is a true-to-life book, a soul-making book. But unlike tidy fiction, it has no plot. My life and soul have no plot—only themes. Here are themes of flight, as in music, as in a fugue.

When I wrote these themes into form some years ago, I was on the way. I was up in the air. My only map was faith. I had embarked on a destiny journey with no idea of my destination. I was telling a true story, but I was in the dark about its plot, its external details, and its resolution. Now some of these have been revealed because I have lived through them. At the outset, I need to tell you some of the missing details, to illuminate what was obscure to me and to fill in the gaps for us both.

The light breaks through into what is essential for me— the sweet and stinging divine Mystery. The book begins and ends with words rendered in new and old forms, telling in subtle and strong language that for God darkness and light are both alike. When God's light breaks forth in human life it can appear as uttermost darkness as well as dazzling brightness, and it can take the form of a blinding fog in between. Nothing tells of this essential mystery better than Psalm 139, which is what comes before the beginning of the book and after its ending as well. If my small human life on earth is a parenthesis in God's eternity, then I want versions of this psalm to form the brackets that hold me.

When I had no idea where I was going, this psalm gave me wings.

The facts are these: I was born at Emanuel Hospital in Portland, Oregon, in the spring of 1947. I grew as a child of the mountains, the forest, the rivers, and the sea. At the age of twenty-one, I left my home for university education in the Midwest. Immediately, I felt cut off from the sources of my life, as if I were in exile. This separation continued for about fourteen years. Each choice I made led to two others, all of them costing one price: *home*. The choices were all exceptionally good, but high-priced. I do not regret one of them. But, until my return, I never ceased to regret losing my sense of place. Once I asked a friend, rhetorically, "How can we survive our choices?" Years later, the answer burst out of me, and practically my first words to this same friend when we met again were, "By learning from them!"

When I was away from home on earth, I learned how much *place* meant to me. It was only in my return and reflection in that sacred place that I learned the limitless importance of *people* in my life. The themes of my sense of exile and homecoming are present in this book, but locked inside them are deeper themes of which I had barely an inkling at the time of writing.

I was an only child, and acquired the strong instinct for solitude that characterizes the only child's survival. It was a surprise to me and to my friends and family that I broke through my solitude at the age of twenty-three by falling in love with Phil and marrying him four days after I was ordained as the first woman deacon in the Episcopal Church in Oregon. We were married at the foot of the Mountain—*my* Mountain, the one I call Angel Mountain in this book, whose public names are Wy'East and Mt. Hood. Marrying Phil was the best thing I ever did for myself. His gifts to me were boundless. His love, his sparkle, his warmth, his outgoing energy, his playfulness, his anger, his music, his perception, his intuition, and above all, his steadfast faithfulness. From him I learned, often painfully, to be at ease with myself and to accept my own contradictions and complexity. And I learned that loving another meant challenging the beloved. Our marriage was totally dynamic and alive. It was sometimes stormy, sometimes despairing, but always a dance, always a blessing.

How I resisted relationship! I refused to view myself as a wife. I was a woman, an autonomous being, an individuating soul. To submit to the narrow cultural definition of wife was reprehensible to me. I insisted that Phil and I refer to each other as "spouse" to indicate our freedom from preconceived roles. We agreed that we wanted to discover and create a unique marriage as we grew into it together.

The truth is, as much as I admired and adored Phil for his person and his gifts, I felt overshadowed. My parents had both been prominent lights, stars in their fields, and now I had married another star. Of course, to my disbelief, Phil said that he sometimes felt the same about me! The emotional insecurity each of us brought to our erotic partnership chafed at us. But we were both determined, even when the dance became a wrestling match—not between potential victors, but between mutually strengthening partners, each other's teachers. Phil was an extroverted, naturally outpouring public person, charismatic both in the popular and theological senses of the word. I was an introverted dreamer, a private mystic, a passionate but intimate friend and lover. In Phil's great public light I sometimes felt invisible. In my intimate radiance, he sometimes felt inadequate or insignificant. We struggled far more against ourselves and our hurt feelings than we did against each other. For my part, the struggle was intensified by the differences in our size. Phil was sixteen inches taller than me and weighed exactly twice as much! We were never able to dance cheek to cheek, only nose to navel. But still, we were an attractive couple, and we were good together because of our differences. We both knew it, too. So we stayed together not only for the joy of loving each other, but for the priceless treasure of what we could learn.

In 1974, Phil and his wonderful mother, Betty, came with me to Philadelphia where I was ordained a priest with ten other women. That was the beginning of a very public emergence for me, which, oddly I suppose, took me by surprise again. After the gift of himself, the second greatest gift Phil gave me was his family. It is quite indescribable. I shouldn't have come through the last fifteen years at all well if I had been deprived of their love and loyalty.

It was in a special turbulence, then, that I began to write this book, for it was just at a time when I had torn myself away from those who loved me most on earth. All of this in my driving need to come home to the land not only that I loved, but that was indeed the land of my soul, my spirit's country. Because my life with Phil from the beginning meant living away from Oregon, I entered our marriage with a divided heart. His natural resistance to uproot himself met my resistance to share myself fully in our marriage. I remained spiritually, and in some ways emotionally, reserved. I resisted the gifts that Phil was eager to share all around us in the natural environment of Minnesota. Phil resisted leaving his known world and coming to Oregon with me. Loneliness began to divide us.

When Phil realized how deep a need I had, he agreed to break through his resistances and to move with me, but by then I was no longer sure that I felt married enough to him to deserve or ask such a radical change of him. I did not want him to feel the resentment of a sacrifice not freely given, as I had come to feel.

In the winter when this book was born, I was grieving, a bear in a protective cave of private confusion. My father had died the year before, and my mother had been gone since shortly after our wedding. I was reflecting on the beautiful spiritual legacy my parents had left me, and feeling at the same time quite orphaned. Moreover, I had bought property in Oregon with my inheritance, and accompanied by Betty, my new mother-by-marriage and friend, I had taken possession of it on July 1 of the preceding summer. Phil and I had agreed to travel back and forth between Oregon and Minnesota until he could get a job as parish priest in the Portland area. We knew that this could take a year or even longer. We also knew that I needed time to sort out the confusion that had grown in my heart. The distance between our spirits that had developed in the last years led me to question whether or not I was married to the right person, whether or not I could experience fulfillment with him, and whether or not I should be married at all. Our tender love and respect for each other had not wavered, but our passionate desire to be together had dimmed in the darkness of my divided heart.

Phil encouraged me to use my solitude in Oregon to explore what I needed and wanted. When we were together, we talked and talked about it. This went on for two years. On top of the stress of our situation, I was experiencing a series of dreams which I felt I had to keep secret from Phil. They were dreams about his death. The first one came at nine o'clock in the morning of March 9, 1982, when I was conducting a retreat for my Wisdom House community in northern Minnesota at the vacation home of one of the women in the community. I woke up sobbing, for in my dream I had seen Phil drift away from me and out of his own body. He couldn't speak, but he smiled and communicated spiritually to me: "It's all right, Honey. It doesn't hurt. It's peaceful! I'm all right. I love you." Then he left. I was beside myself.

I began to have dreams about my father's death as well. My father died six months after the dreams began, on October 22. The dreams about him stopped, but the dreams about Phil continued. I never told him, but I shared my anguish and confusion with close friends. And I cried copiously and secretly. Were these dreams precognitive and literal, as the dreams about my father had been, or were they a metaphor of the deep and painful transformation we were experiencing in our marriage? I had no way of knowing, so I responded like a person who had been dealt two hands, not knowing which one she would have to play in the draw. I prepared both hands—the literal and the metaphoric—as fully as I could.

On the metaphoric level, I committed myself with deep determination to work as hard as I could to find the truth about us. Did we belong together? Could I achieve the complete emotional honesty necessary to give our marriage its chance for fulfillment? Could I overcome my unfair protective feelings toward Phil which had kept me from telling him what I really needed and wanted in a lover, out of my fear of hurting his feelings, or of being disappointed? Could Phil, who had been my first and best playmate, become my true soulmate? Did I have the right to ask for the changes that might make that possible? On the literal level, the questions were equally hard. Could I bear his death? Could I be widow as well as orphan and still want to live? How would I feel if he died with all that was unfinished between us? Should I simply leave him first, to avoid the anguishing possibility of him leaving me in death? Slowly, I began to work out these questions, first by practicing being honest in sharing my darker feelings and deeper needs with Phil, and then by introducing the subject of our deaths by expressing feelings about my own death. This enabled us to explore more and more fully and deeply what each of us most longed for in life and from each other, and what we thought and felt about our own deaths. It was the hardest and most rewarding work either of us had ever done. I didn't address it directly in this book, because I was too much in the midst of it to understand it fully or to be able to describe it, and because my book wasn't about marriage, but about healing and creativity. I was living through the breaking of my own light into shards of opacity, sharp and mysterious to me, and writing the book was a lifeline—a spiritual anchor, an enactment of my deepest need to heal myself through a creative process which reintegrated my spiritual, emotional, and intellectual powers at a time of apparent disintegration in my life. The creative process became my link with integrity as I struggled for it in the most intimate aspects of my life.

Now, in the afterlight of experience, it seems important that I reveal what was happening more specifically in my life and soul at the time of giving forth the reflections that follow.

Our work came to a climax a year after I finished this book. It was June, and we were in Oregon together, working again in our garden, which I describe in the "Humus" chapter. Phil had begun a sabbatical summer, and in the spiritual reading which he had done he discerned a new direction for himself. In reading Scott

Peck's now classic *The Road Less Traveled*, Phil realized that spiritual discipline was indeed a gift that he wanted to give to himself. He also convinced me that, since "love is desire for the spiritual growth of the beloved," the most loving thing I could do for him was to challenge him to grow. This meant telling him outright what was missing for me in our marriage! I had entered marriage with the notion that one hasn't the right to ask another to change. So in those areas of our relationship where I felt lonely, I simply had accepted that Phil and I were different, and it was his perfect right not to be like me or able to share with me certain dimensions of experience which were inward and slow. He was outward and fast! Nothing wrong with that.

I had tried to make myself faster and more outgoing to meet him, but there were limits, probably where I felt unreciprocated. We each had unconsciously interpreted these limits as being uncared for. That was not true. The truth was, the limits stopped us at a point of isolation. My acceptance had become resignation, my resignation had become disappointment, my disappointment had become despair, and the despair became a kind of deadness, which is what I unconsciously brought to our marriage. Phil experienced this as my indifference, which it was not! He knew that there were times when I expressed affection to him that I did not feel, and more often times when I expressed nothing at all. In finding the courage to tell me his feelings of loss and longing, I was able to assure him that I had touched and hugged and kissed him even when I didn't necessarily feel like it, because I believe that he deserved to be touched and hugged and kissed, regardless of my feelings. I told him that I loved him so much and cared so deeply for him that I was committed to working with him when, with anyone else in the world, it would have been too painful to do so. He was glad to hear me say these things, but he also taught me that I had been wrong to disregard my own feelings and needs, and had done him a disservice in simply assuming that he couldn't or wouldn't make an effort to pay attention and meet me where I most needed to be met. He said, "Will you give me a chance to change, and wait for me to discover what a deepening of my own spirituality can mean for us?" I responded, "Of course. But do it for yourself, and not to save our marriage, and then let us see how your spiritual renewal affects us." And he did!

Over the next few months, after finding a place of utmost honesty and courage together, Phil opened himself to a new inner world, and he became personally transformed, even transfigured. A new radiance, soul-deep and lasting, became visible through his being. He was truly enthused—God-filled—and eager not only to share with me the world of dreams and meditation, but he actually brought a brand new spiritual richness into our marriage, teaching me things that had been harmonious with my interests but in the past of little interest to him personally. With what joy I learned from Phil how to do a "Zen Walk" on our living room carpet! And so, the attention and time for which I had longed in our marriage came forth in greater measure than I imagined possible, and the outpouring of my affection toward Phil was not only felt and spontaneous, but nonstop! We had, after fifteen years, truly married each other. And for six months of bliss and infinite mutual patience, encouragement, and loving nurture, our honeymoon went on. Now with no further need to defend my autonomy, since it was so dearly cherished and respected by my soulmate, I was able to declare myself a woman who was also a wife, knowing that it meant the beloved and mutual partner of my husband. We had persevered in the hard work of living deeply and fully together and after intense struggle we had broken through a kind of finish line. We were looking forward to sharing the next thirty years enjoying the sweet fruit of our long labor together.

Then, after I had almost forgotten about the old anguishing dreams, on the morning of December 9, at nine o'clock, Phil died. He was a perfectly healthy thirty-seven-year-old man, who had a slight cold, and who woke up on Monday morning not knowing that his lungs were filled with blood clots. He felt weak and dizzy, and a few minutes later he simply stopped breathing. The medical team worked for over an hour to bring him back to his body, but they could not know at the time that there simply was no room for air in his lungs. No one can explain how this happened, except to say that the virus that had caused his sniffles may have suddenly caused his blood to coagulate. It was fast, painless, and peaceful, as he had promised me in the first dream, three years and nine months to the minute earlier. I did not know it at the time, but as I wrote this book I was experiencing a kind of death-pregnancy. Elsewhere, I have written about my healing process since then, so I will not go into that here.

This book is not about death. It is about life, which

includes death; about creation, which includes destruction. It is about the essential oneness of all that is. It is about the comforting mystery of that oneness. It is about the irrepressible light born in the dark heart of our brokenness and brought forth by the God of All.

Now I invite you to read on, to accompany me through the mystery. Take heart. The following chapters will not be as hard for either of us as this one has been. Remember, I did not know where I was going when I wrote them!

### Equinox

Waiting for the first clap
of September thunder,
waiting for the silver
birch to turn to gold,
waiting for the unknown,
waiting for the unforeseen. . . .
The journey continues unceasingly,
a journey into beginnings.

### Solstice

Winter waits like a woman
pregnant with possibility
while the fish in my dreams
swim toward the light. . . .

Waiting.
Into the dark with its holy
sounds, its secret holdings.
Into the quiet tunnel of despair
through which understanding comes,
and joy, in knowing
that we cannot understand.

Holy One, you have searched me out and known me;
you know my sitting down and my rising up;
you discern my thoughts from afar.

You trace my journeys and my resting-places
and are acquainted with all my ways.

Indeed, there is not a word on my lips,
but you, O God, know it altogether.

You press upon me behind and before
and lay your hand upon me.

Such knowledge is too wonderful for me;
it is so high that I cannot attain to it.

Where can I go then from your Spirit?
Where can I flee from your presence?

If I climb up to heaven, you are there;
if I make the grave my bed, you are there also.

If I take the wings of the morning
and dwell in the uttermost parts of the sea,

Even there your hand will lead me
and your right hand hold me fast.

If I say, "Surely the darkness will cover me,
and the light around me turn to night,"

Darkness is not dark to you;
the night is as bright as the day;
darkness and light to you are both alike.

For you yourself created my inmost parts;
you knit me together in my mother's womb.

I will thank you because I am marvelously made;
your works are wonderful, and I know it well.

My body was not hidden from you,
while I was being made in secret
and woven in the depths of the earth.

Your eyes beheld my limbs, yet unfinished in the womb;
all of them were written in your book;
they were fashioned day by day,
when as yet there was none of them.

How deep I find your thoughts, O God!
How great is the sum of them!

If I were to count them, they would be more in number
than the sand; to count them all, my life span
would need to be like yours. . . .

> from Psalm 139
> adapted from *The Book of Common Prayer*, 1979

*O you works of God bless your God,*
*give praise and glory forever.*
              *The Book of Daniel*

*In my beginning is my end. . . .*
              T. S. Eliot

*One*
# The Mountain

She is my Medicine Woman. In the morning when the earth turns so that the sun again smiles over her white shoulder, I call her Angel Mountain. She is two million years old, she and her ancestor mountain whose bones can still be seen on her north face. It is her west face that she shows to me. I live in her ocean-facing shadow.

Tonight in mild midwinter the moon has risen full over her snow-heightened frame. She stands out majestic and white in the moon-softened indigo sky. She is Queen of the Night. I gaze through the darkness toward her healing face, as I have gazed through the day. The moon's penumbra sends out equal beams of light to the four cardinal points of the universe, an equal-armed cross signifying wholeness, the enfolding expansion in all directions, the unfolding from the core: all light comes from and returns to the Source. Below, the names I know of the Mountain's body shine: Steel Cliff, a shadow on her south shoulder, now iron rose, and Illumination Rock, a peaceful glimmer in a solitary sky. I do not know the names of the left side of her west face. The left is secret. The side of the soul. This Mountain, too, has soul. She teaches me what it means to be a creature, true to creation. She is alive. Her heart still rumbles. Her breath smokes out from cracks on her surface. She wakes and sleeps. In human history she moves slowly, but in her own time, her breath never falters.

She teaches me what can be made of light.

All day I wait patiently for the clouds to climb around her body so that I can see it again, see how their play changes her. The mists roll on her rocks like furry grey cubs. They leave shadow marks like visible kisses. Light cuts ridges into places I have never seen before, though I've looked each day of my life. This two-million-year-old creature ceaselessly changes.

Angel Mountain makes me wait for change. Wait for my vision to clear. Wait for confusion of clouds to pass. Wait for rain to end. Wait for wonder.

I remember what John, my priest-shaman, said to me before I left Minnesota for my Oregon home in deep winter: "Your life is an unfolding mystery. What you do now is a mystery. You are making choices whose meaning only the future can reveal. You cannot explain yourself to your friends. You cannot explain yourself to yourself. No one can understand. Each one will make whatever meaning of it that is right and true for that person. Your silence, too, can be loving, true to the gift of your life. You must go to your Mountain, your Jerusalem, to discover who you are in your Holy Place.

Your friends bless you and pray for you, entrusting you to the Way which you yourself must come to trust. We will miss you, but we know you must go. Do not carry your pain alone on your journey. Let your Creator carry it for you."

The Mountain also carries my pain. The Mountain is luminous. She illuminates my pain. She is a companion creature, sharing time and space in a common place. She is older and stronger than I, a semi-active volcano, wise in her ways, true to herself in her freedom from the need to understand. I stand under her, unable to understand my own mystery or pain, yet here in this sacred stillness I receive an inkling of the meaning of my journey. In the play of shadow and light, withdrawal and sudden emergence, as I witness her volcanic agonies, I sense that I, too, am part of a meaningful Whole. I come to love my role. I come to love even my own folly, and to trust in the wisdom that gives harmony to the deepest cries of creation giving birth and being born. All light breaks against form. Some light breaks through into new forms. I will sit here and learn to do *my job of becoming well*: resting, relaxing, recovering myself, under the rainbow wings of moonlight breaking through crystal prisms in my living room window, under the Mountain, my Medicine Woman, my Mother.

\* \* \*

This afternoon after waiting for four hours, I watched her re-emerge through my binoculars. I had taken a bath at noon, not a long bath, and when I returned to the winter window, she was gone! I had wasted the morning expecting to have a leisurely afternoon with her. After all these years I still have to learn the daily lesson: take nothing for granted. So at last, at four o'clock, the thinning clouds romped behind her and uncurled themselves from her form. As much as my eyes thirsted for her, they kept wandering around on the foothills and foreground meadows, to cavort with the neighboring animals: she-goat and her thwarted paramour ram, young black steer, nibbling deer, grey geese, roosters, and horses—all at-home against the backdrop of wedgewood blue house and barn under blue spruce trees. House and barn belong to my neighbors, the Trosts. Suddenly I caught an intrusive shadow on the Japanese maple shrub beneath my window. A human visitor! Shyly, the woman and man let me welcome them. They expected to see the old couple who built this blessed house for their retirement, and were bewildered to find a solitary young woman instead. "They moved nearer to their children and sold the place to me," I explained.

"We came to see your rock pond, and the Mountain. May we?" I was glad to have guests who recognized the beauty of the large and varied agate and lava forms, thunder eggs, and petrified wood and quartz, which my predecessors had shaped into the stone wall and water fountain on the property. I regretted that the magnolia tree and hundred rhododendrons were still tightly in bud this February day. When the people left they noticed my Minnesota license plate that reads "BEAR UP."

"Is your family in Minnesota?"

"No. My family is here." I felt surprised, as if I had betrayed my own kin without knowing it in time, and the strangers left before I had time to explain myself . . . to myself and them. I wanted to say, "My closest relatives are dead, but my family is here. My friends are my family now. The human friends and relatives can write or visit or telephone, and I can drive or fly to see them. But these friends remain in one place. I have to place myself in their presence—the Mountain, the Ocean, the River, the Forest, the Waterfalls. I belong to them. I depend on them for my healing and growth. They heal by teaching me to remember who I am."

But I was not given time to explain, so I simply returned to my work of sitting at the foot of the Mountain and listening to what I see.

### Here through There

Weather in Athens and Tel Aviv
is better than here. The Negev
is still warm, light still dazzles
the white beaches of Greece.

To Jerusalem, then,
with only the necessary,
my body and three books:

Thomas Merton translates
Chinese poetry, Kinnell's
new verse in *The Past*;
and a saga of Psyche,
*On the Way to the Wedding*.

What travel aids I need

are locked inside.
I have been this year
lost from myself.

The harder I look
the less I find.
I will abandon looking
and let myself see.

Hence this deep sea journey:

I go to the Holy Land,
To the Place of Blessing within.

# Two
# Neighbors

My eyes are trying to eat a mountain for breakfast.
They are in competition with a cloud, greedily devouring the mid-section of its morning meal on the horizon.
My eyes are winning.

Looking is like eating. It can't be done all at once.
First a bite, then the distracted chewing, the thorough
swallow, the idle interspersing commentary. It is a
rhythm, in order to prevent choking and engorgement.
So my eye is constantly pulled away from its purpose,
seduced by the foreground. I am called to attend to
what is near me. To keep from blurring my vision with
a fixation of focus, I allow my eyes their natural
movement, their inclination to scan. I regard the fairy
castle in the sky, the tricky fantasy of nature having its
way with me, promising no view of the Mountain this
occluded morning, and then, suddenly, a gleaming
triangle appears, breaking through grey gauze. It seems

to turn, rocky cliffs becoming magical towers holding wizards and visions in secret windows and mirrors of ice. It has no foundation whatever, but floats majestically and freely in a watery sky. It is held in space only by an ancient Douglas fir tree that stands in midground to the north, a green pinnacle the fairy rulers use as a ladder to reach their royal home. I want to trace the changes as they occur, knowing that duration is not part of the promise and everything may disappear for days, and I may never see the Mountain in just this way again. But my eye drifts, itself lost in a cloud of dimmed consciousness. I watch the three horses lying in the open meadow—Aga Khan and Reno who are nearly thirty years old, and young Rocky, my human neighbor Misty's colt. My eye is enchanted to see them rolling like puppies on their backs, treading the air with all fours. I think of calling Misty's mother Melody to ask if this is normal equine behavior!

Meanwhile, the Mountain fantasy is dissolving! I am wasting the vision! Finally I have to admit that it is impossible to keep my focus fixed on a white triangle floating in space, even if my passionate eye is both hungry and in love. Beholder and beheld need freedom to place the imaged encounter in context. That apparent straying from the image of the beloved is really reflection and assimilation, absolutely necessary to the endurance of the relationship.

Three eagles fly over the old fir tree toward the Mountain's summit, and I remember that my castle is really a live volcano in winter sleep. I remember seeing a solitary eagle circle my garden last summer at sunset and thinking of the image of God, bearing us up "as on eagle's wings"—like a mother eagle teaching her young to fly. She leaves the eyrie with her children on her outstretched wings, then lowers her wings to let them feel their own. Each day she lets them know more and more of their own strength, raising her wings to uphold them when they tire. Then the day arrives when they are ready to fly on their own, and she soars off into her own new life as her children do. Should she fail to let them go, grown children unable to fly would weight down their mother's wings so that she also would be grounded, and all would die. So we take our lesson in human relationships, and look to the powers given us by our loving Creator to let our own spirits soar. And I remember more.

I remember an early autumn hike to Ramona Falls, long closed for the snow season. Then it was a journey through fairyland, rain-kissed wild pink rhododendrons and moss-covered rocks tracing the miles up the Mountain to one of her secret treasures. Then the Falls themselves—rainbow falls, because light eased through the evergreen trees to play on the black lava folds like organ pipes, in shards of layered color.

I am impatient for spring and the flowers' return. I smile at my Old Trickster Mountain and return my eye to the part of earth nearest me and plan where I will throw wildflower seeds in front of the fruit trees in my own meadow in March.

I also remember a picture I took of the Mountain last year, standing for ten minutes in the middle of the highway waiting for the best view from Laurel Hill. I

9

braced myself in a curve on the yellow line and blessed the cars that didn't come that way for that time. Then, in the three seconds of clarity that were given that day, I took the picture. The Mountain looked like an eye: softly diamond-shaped with a protrusion of dark trees in the center of finely veined white. It was the filled iris of a gigantic Awakening Eye, looking at me. I named the picture *Cosmic Eye-con*.

## At the End of this Road

The dream says wait
by not-waiting.
Enter fog fully,
give yourself
to the cloud
completely.

Go to the white summit
and then turn around,
not to go back but
to see the other side
of yourself and the whole
path by which you brought
yourself here. Then hold
to the Mountain. Stay
until morning.

Drink what warmth
the dazzling gives.
Eat light like a leaf
and be transfigured.

Learn all the secrets
the snowy desert
can teach you in one
incarnation.

Do not think you are
waiting for another part
of your life to begin.

Be intrigued, be overwhelmed
where you are, taking time
to note how everything comes to
you unbidden to meet your desire.

Cultivate not-waiting.
Learn the new speech
that thin air makes.

Where you are is
nearly over and
is always. Wait
without waiting.

*Three*
# My Eye

I do not have a calculating eye, only a loving one. When I stood in the middle of the highway waiting for the cloud bank to open around my future picture, it was love and faith that held me, not the power of prediction. I am hourly astonished by the gift of surprise that the Mountain brings—for pleasure or pain, in revelation or withdrawal. I cannot, nor can anyone, forecast her moods. She is more autonomous than the weather. Her disposition is more akin to human than to any other. For this reason, I can more easily admit that I cannot calculate human tendencies much better than can my eye the Mountain's. She has taught me to remain open to the unexpected moments when life erupts and everything changes, the moments when human needs emerge. We call these moments emergencies. They are never indicated on the calendar.

My telephone rang at midnight. When someone has gone to the country to write and retreat, such interruptions might seem rare and unwelcome. My friends across the country know that I am a night creature, so here the midnight visitor catches my prime attention. I must say that this visit was unusual and unhappy, although a redemptive image broke through in time. Someone I knew in my other life, during my friendly exile in the Midwest, called to tell me that she had a facial tumor which was to be removed surgically next week and very likely would result in major nerve damage, perhaps in partial paralysis of the left side of her face. My heart went out to Laurie. What comfort could I possibly offer, how could I help her prepare? There had already been a recent meaningful connection between us. She had written to me the week before to tell me about her friend, a Roman Catholic Sister, who is in mortal combat with cancer. The Sister and I have never met, but I immediately offered to unite my energy with hers each Thursday, when she visualizes healing in her body. Last week was my first to pray with the two women across two thousand miles. Two days later, the Sister got on a city bus in Minneapolis and sat next to a stranger who proceeded spontaneously to read her a poem of mine. Our connection was secured. Now our mutual friend who has solicited my prayers for another woman was in trouble herself. I felt useless.

Then I remembered something. Something obvious that I consequently keep forgetting. When Laurie said to me, "Alla, why my *face*?" I said, "I don't know. Do you remember *my* face?"

"Your face is beautiful."

"My left eyelid droops."

"What?"

"Try to remember what I really look like."

"Well, I guess I noticed it at first, but I'd forgotten. I don't see it anymore."

"That's how it will be with you if your nerve is damaged in the operation. I've had nine operations on my eye since it was injured at birth. At first people notice and sometimes they ask about it. Children always do. I tell them, 'It was hurt when I was a baby, but I can see just fine, and it doesn't hurt me anymore.' Then they get to know me and forget about it. You'll be just like me, and that's not so bad! We'll both have long brown hair and a sexy droop on the left!"

She laughed and said I'd always been her role model, so this unusual similarity between us might not be such a disaster after all. Thank God. I had remembered an old scar that I could light up and turn momentarily into a tool, maybe even a beauty mark.

I sit here in the gloaming, grateful that I remembered my gift in time last night, and I laugh at my own unusually literal self-description of several years ago, as I sit watching a streak of alpenglow mauve on the Mountain and sunset on the lower ridges at the same time without shifting both eyes:

### Double-sighted Mantra

My nose
is a bridge
between
East and West

Mystery lady, oriental on the left, occidental on the right: I can enjoy being unpredictable. My ecumenical face.

*Four*
# Emmaus

There is a town near here called Damascus. I used to drive through it early in the morning on my way to classes. The sun would blind me on the east-facing curves of that road. I thought of the conversion of Saul on the road to Damascus in another time and another part of the world. He was thrown on the ground by sheer light alone, and the light spoke to him. It told him to go to a certain place and wait for guidance. He was converted from leading himself by ego and will to listening to the light within, to waiting on the light, to serving the light. His conversion, apt for one who ruled others by the power of sight, was blinding. He had to wait in darkness and entrust himself to the vision and voices of others.

In order to have our sight renewed we sometimes have to endure the dark. For one third of our lives, sleep overtakes us and rests our eyes, closing out light and form until our organs of sight are restored by rest.

Our eyes are quiet while we sleep, except when we dream, and our dreams comfort us in the void. When we awaken refreshed, our vision, too, is restored. We can see in the day. Each meeting between seer and seen holds the chance for new meaning. Mutual focus creates a true scene. You see me and I see you. In the same moment we are each both seer and seen. (In the meeting between, the question emerges: *how* do you *mean*?)

I began to play with the scenario of meeting and seeing last spring when I accepted an invitation for the second time to speak on the subject of spirituality in the School of Medicine at Stanford University. I was again gratified that scientists were eager for engagement with the feeling side of healing, but I had no idea what to say. So I began to explore my own problem: How can I focus? What *is* focusing? An avid word detective, I went to my source— the dictionary. In Latin, the *focus* is—the hearth! The family fireplace. The heart of the home. Now meaning was rampant and we were off and flying.

What happens at the hearth? People gather together to share light and warmth, to bake and break bread, and to partake of the family stewpot that nourishes all the senses. Occasionally when an individual cannot sleep or feels creative or meditative in the middle of the night or early morning hours, the hearth is a place to come in solitude to seek renewal as well as comfort. People tell each other stories around the hearth, share the power of laughter and tears. People sit in silent reflection together in the dancing light of the fire. The hearth is a place of communion and communication, of comfort and companionship. It nurtures and nourishes our solitude and our solidarity.

Fire and light lead to the receptive qualities of reflection and refraction. The human eye reflects and refracts: if I look into your eye, I find my own image reflected in the light playing there; and at the same moment, my image is refracted within your eye in order for you to recognize me. I went to the word book to find the specific meanings of these properties. A mirror reflects, a lens refracts. The eye can be a mirror for others on the outside, but inside is a lens for personal purpose. To refract means "to break through." Seeing occurs when light breaks through the lens to form a clear image within the eye. This image is called the real focus, parallel to the virtual focus which is the seen reality in its own place outside the eye. When the lens is covered by a cataract, something has broken down over the eye and no light can break through into an image inside.

In modern physics there is a theory that the entire universe is made of light, that the tiny quanta called photons, or particles of light, compose every palpable, visible aspect of creation, including the human eye. Light is not only the means of seeing but the seeing itself. Darkness is not the absence of light, but a property of light: its inner density. Darkness is the inside-out of light, the self-revelation of the heart of the photon. Darkness is the essence of light, essential to clear vision. If everything were made of equal light, had the same proportion of shadow and intensity, we could not distinguish one thing from another. We would be blind in an amorphous brightness, and no thing could show its meaning, its self.

So in the psalms the singer voices the nature of the Creator to whom the darkness and light are both alike and the night is as clear as the day. The night's clarity is an inner clarity. It is only in the night that we know we are not alone in the universe, but surrounded by galaxies of witnesses whose lights come to us in the stars and planets of the cosmos. Because our dwellings are illuminated at night by candlepower in one form or another, we make night-time in our homes the outside-in of day. All is a play in the cosmic shadow-dance. My own darkness is part of this.

Sometimes it is in experiencing my own darkness most deeply that I am most aware and appreciative of the lights of others. The darkness deep down within is the place where life begins. If everything alive began as a dream that was loved into waking being, then night is the true origin of everything. When dreams break through into our conscious life we can see what we truly feel and mean. When plants break through the earth and emerge in the field of our vision, we have an inkling of future beauty and nurture.

For your image to form in my life, I have to allow your light to break through the lens of my experience in order to make a clear meaning within my *I*. I have to uncover and open my *I* in order to see you truly and fully. If seeing is power, the beginning of accurate movement in response and in mutual giving and receiving, then my power is possible only when I am uncovered and open. My eye, my inner *I*, opens to show me that there is a real world outside me which also includes me, and my *I* closes and rests in order to show trust in what I have seen and to take its truth into my being. I lean into the larger life and allow myself to fall into sleep confident that it will continue to contain me. This is also the way in which I fall into love, or fall into God: I see that an Other exists, and I am filled from within by the beauty and meaning of this recognition, knowing that the loving Other I see, also sees me.

Falling into sleep, falling into love, falling into God: all predicate a letting go, a faith in the Unknown, the easy, spontaneous surrender of the self in total trust.

It was Eastertime when these ideas rose in my mind. I happened to read the Gospel story of the Risen Christ walking unrecognized with two companions on the road to Emmaus. It became clear to me how it could happen. They could not *see* a reality of which they had never dreamed. "Are you the only one in Jerusalem who doesn't know what has happened in the past three days?" As the three figures walked together, Christ heard the story of his own death from two strangers. He then told them stories from the prophets to illuminate the events, but explanations did not help them to recognize their companion. It was only when they stopped to share a meal together that something truly changed their perception: Christ broke bread with them, and their eyes were opened. And so we return to the hearth. The bread of life was broken between three storytellers, and suddenly the meanings formed within them all at once. The bread and the simple, necessary act of breaking it, gave them a focus, so that the light of Christ could finally break through the lens of their experience of walking on the road together. The lonely limitations of their expectations were broken through, and their vision expanded to include a new reality: "It is possible to rise from the dead, and we know this now because we have seen and heard one whose experience we can now recognize. Not in our efforts to communicate, but in our silent communion of the common need for food, and in breaking bread and sharing the response to that need, our eyes were filled with the truth, and our hearts were on fire with the light of what we saw."

> I invite and long for
> your light to break through me
> so that I can see
> what you mean.
>
> I live to break through
> into your meaning too,
> so that we can share
> the Bread of Life
> together.

I was back in Minnesota at Christmastime. It was thirty degrees below zero on Christmas Eve. Only two people came to midnight Mass at which I was priest and celebrant in the attic chapel of our home. I sat between the two congregants and wrapped my priestly stole around their shoulders, to share ministry and (symbolic) warmth. We huddled near the heater beside the altar as the animals must have huddled around the birth scene in the barn.

All three of us were on the brink of something new and unknown in our lives. Our trembling was from cold, from beauty, and from fear. But we warmed each other, sitting close, and quietly taking in the candlelight of the most magical night of the year, just after the winter solstice when the earth turns again toward her star and days of longer light, and the Creator becomes *incarnate* as a child in our midst.

Our eyes focused on the altar, a physical structure which happened to have a narrow slit in its center. It was through this slit that our eyes were pulled as we shared the image of birth in our meditation after the Gospel. The Word of God that is the origin of everything, that called all being into being, became small, took on the limitations that we ourselves know. We remembered what it was like to be born: to fight our way into life or die, to pass through the tight place, out from the holy dark of our mothers' bodies into the confusing light of a larger world. We remembered how little we could see when we were born. Falling up into the Unknown, only the familiar warmth of the mother's body still safely there for us, we found ourselves in complete disequilibrium, totally confused. All forms were equally foreign. We could see nothing, for nothing as yet had context. It was a time before meaning, like no time at all. Gradually we began to see as we entered into and formed relationships: first with the outside of the mother's body as we were fed at her breast, then with her face as we were nurtured by her caring eyes and smile, and slowly, with the faces of others.

Little by little, as we came to touch our world, we began to see, and then to name, the parts of it. Seeing is a consequence of being born, and of being reborn. Seriously premature babies may be blind. It is important to be born in one's own time. And resurrection cannot be willed. The flower that blooms longest is not the one that was forced open. Seeing well means meeting in the same moment: seer and seen, borne together by the meaning of true meeting. And every eye-opening is a beginning. Christmas and Easter are always only the beginning and the rebeginning. And our vision grows as we break bread and give thanks together.

## Photography: Light-writing

The body,
a brief visitor,
a moment's miracle,
a material gift
in the trade
of dancing
particle and wave.

Light, captured
by melanin into
the black hole
of the body,
escapes, becomes
itself again,

leaving the body,
beloved's body,
in a burst
beyond ecstasy:

This picture I took
of you in Wildwood
by the river sitting
in the dead body
of a cedar stump,
arms thrown open,
head upward, exultant,
sundrenched with
the forest, alive,
your whole being
hugging the Light!

*Five*
# The White Deer

I don't like suffering. When I first came here, for the first time in my life I *suffered* solitude. It was because I felt guilty for having left my friends and family to renew myself. Then I felt embarrassed for feeling guilty, because everyone had blessed me in my going. Everyone who loved me had assured me that, though they would miss me and were momentarily angry at my going, they knew that I needed time alone, and they wished me well. My main weakness of feeling overly responsible for others had once again thwarted me. All my life I may have to work to transform this distortion of feeling into the purer, more realistic detachment of being responsible *to* others and responsible *for* myself as we grow into mutuality.

Now over time I have opened myself to the gift of acceptance which my friends and family have given me. Each day I open my pretty, white rural mailbox with its flying birds—cardinals, goldfinches, chickadees—and receive messages that help me to accept acceptance. My kitchen windowsill is filled with cards and wordflowers from friends far and near, insistent with acceptance: electric blue irises from my artist friend, Julia; unicorns and bears and a Pegasus from Godchildren and soul-mates; a mountain lake from new neighbors welcoming me; and today, a Mayan picture-card from Melissa, whom I helped to ordain, on her wildflower safari in the breathtaking jungles of Belize, and a textile scene of a mountain moonrise with messages of spring flowers from Sandra, exploring ministry in Minnesota. Yesterday, a Valentine gift of an essay by Owen Barfield came from my intellectual resource and friend Jo, who today called me long distance to describe her amazing new computer—just as I happened to be listening to meditation music she had given me before Christmas. I am surrounded by icons of my friends' love for me. I find them irresistible. Thus overwhelmed, how can I still stubbornly refuse so much love in favor of my poor and precious guilt? I surrender. I have allowed their blessing to break through and touch me. And I am blessed indeed.

Last night I consulted the *I Ching* for inner counsel, and the current oracle came up as "The Creative, Heaven": blessing will come from the depths of the universe to help you to choose between the demands of the public hero or the secluded sage, according to the needs of your innermost being now.

I embrace my seclusion and I am ready to learn.

It is a pregnant time for me. I am pregnant with the future in a focused way. I am pregnant with choice. I yearned for this pregnancy, yet, at times, and even now, I dread it. I do not like the loss of the familiar: my familiar body, my familiar habits. So many changes give way to make room for new life. Then there is the suffering of wait. Of weight and wait. I am heavy with something I do not yet know, have not yet named, and I grow different each day because of it. I long for it to reveal itself. I long to give it a name. Yet I do not know what it is. I must wait on the will of heaven and discern how best to respond and move with it moment by moment. Thank God that pregnancy is temporary. Thank God birth comes, and labor, too, is limited. Such intensity is not something to be prolonged. Birth has its private and public phases. It is my private time: the final heaviness and discomfort, the panting for life, the bleeding. Later comes the public time: the proclaiming of a name in the presence of those who have promised to love me, the celebration and blessing of what has been born(e).

Meanwhile, I surrender to the demands of the time, and to my own needs. I adjust to my new environment, acquaint myself with my neighbors, am soothed by soft Oregon rain gently tap dancing on my roof. After several days of the latter, my neighbor Arty called from her Galloping Goose Ranch, which is my main visual entertainment from the kitchen window when I tire of writing. "Alla, my ewes are ready to give birth. Come see the new lambs when you get tired of the rain. You know, I recently read that sunshine stimulates a naturally euphoric hormone in the body. I'm about ready for a shot of it!"

Arty and her family went skiing, and the lambs were born while they were away—three sets of twins: two white, two black, and two black-and-white woollies. One incredibly sunny day, filled with happy hormones and optimism, I strode up the hill to greet the new arrivals. They were as big as Sabrina, the sweet basset who strolls in my meadow! And the scamps were chasing a young rooster—an animal that I had never before seen fly. This one was practically soaring! How quickly the newborn can learn how to live, and challenge others to stretch their own wings!

Well, critters, I am your willing pupil. Teach me to live.

"Alla, we have a new animal in the neighborhood," Melody said, in the same excited tone she had used to tell me her twin grandsons were born around Thanksgiving time. Melody, my neighbor to the south, is pure spunk. "I never would have gotten through my adolescence if the Sisters at St. Rose hadn't turned me around, and if St. Mary Euphrasia hadn't kept her eye on me!" Melody moved me with her generosity last summer, bringing me baskets of flowers and fruit from her garden, and jars full of exquisite jams: rhubarb, spiced peach, and raspberry. Today she brings me hot peanut butter cookies from her oven, and she tells me the news while I make orange tea: "It's a *white deer*."

My city eye is constantly excited by backyard activity here: mountain bluebirds that came to enjoy the rock pond right after I swept out stagnant water and rain refilled it; scrub jays in the brush; Oregon juncos and varied thrush under the bushes; red shafted flickers in the tulip tree; western tanager in the cherry branch; and evening grosbeak under the lilac limbs. In August, we heard, but never saw, coming up from the Sandy River, what sounded to me like an elephant bellowing. My Oregon biohistory book assures me that elephants have not been here at least since the Eocene age. That was a mystery. But whatever it was has come and gone.

Now something new had come to waken us to wonder. A white deer! "Is it an albino?"

"No. It has brown eyes and brown markings where other deer have white."

"Where did you see it?"

"Once in the morning and once in late afternoon driving down Ten Eyck hill, I looked up into the woods and saw it."

That's less than two miles from here. Another neighbor, Norm, told me he saw a small black bear on the road near there in November. Now we have a really rare creature to teach us something old and new under the sun.

Every afternoon I go for a walk and a ride. I drive slowly up Ten Eyck hill and look, but see nothing with my untrained eyes but trees and brush and a few eager buds on bare branches. I drive down the highway toward town, gaze out on the snowquilted lower Cascades, curve around the nearby little ex-volcanoes that now cradle churches and houses and schools peacefully in the sun, and try not to think of the deer. Try not to expect it nor want too much to see it. When I go back down the hill, I turn on the radio and try to be casual and not look up into the woods, as if the white deer were clearly not at home today, or busy with important matters and unavailable, or simply a common enough creature to be able to avoid with no great loss, but it is a lie. I want to see that deer. I am stifling my desire to such a degree that I feel as if I'm falling off the earth. My whole concentration is in making myself detached, light, above the pull of gravity, entirely given to the grip of centrifugal force. I fall out of my car, off the road, off the ridge, off the earth, into the void, in my determination not to mind not seeing the white deer. A little red airplane glides over the hemlock trees. Someone is going up in a bright yellow balloon from a field down the road. Look! Look! I say to myself. But truly I do not care. I want to see that deer. Earthbound and weird. I feel affinity. I climb back on the earth and own my desire. I keep on looking, and no longer hide what I want from myself.

The deer is important to me because it shows in its whole body a mystery I have been growing into for some time. Life is a play of opposites, and at the heart of one thing lives another. The embryo growing in its mother's womb is totally other from her, yet it lives under her heart and grows from her body. I experience this play on a daily basis in relationships. To love and trust another person, and to engage respectfully in mutual growth is constantly to be open to another point of view. Consider having a prolonged argument with a partner, and suddenly in the same inkling, each one sees the other person's point of view and surrenders! It takes more time to complete the situation, because each person is still on the opposite side from the other, although they have both reversed themselves, passing each other in different directions!

Then there are the moments of what one expects to be pure joy or pure sorrow, and right in the middle of it, one feels the opposite: sadness at a wedding, joy at a funeral. I call this the *yin of yang* or the *yang of yin*. The *I Ching*, or *Book of Changes*, is based on it. The elements of life are constantly growing toward their fullest possibility, then changing into their opposite. So the feminine principle, or *yin*, grows and grows until it has entirely fulfilled itself as *old yin*, and at its most extreme moment, it becomes *young yang*. The same holds for the male principle, *yang: old yang* becomes *young yin*.

The graphic symbol for the interflow of *yin* and *yang* is called the *Tao*, which means the *Way*. It is a circle divided by a flowing curved line from top to bottom and left to right. One side of the curve is light and the other side is dark. But what is truly important is this: in the center of the dark side, there is a small circle of pure light, and in the center of the light side, there is a small circle of pure dark. Though so different, each side is intimately known by the other because it contains the other in its core—it holds the other in its heart.

Chinese wisdom literature is not the only source for this reverence for rhythmic transformation, mutual recognition, and interflow. Western scripture also speaks of it in the form of interplay between darkness and light. Jewish mystical tradition celebrates the Sabbath union of the feminine and masculine aspects of the Holy One as the source of all life. The same quality exists in the archetypes of the inner *anima* of each man and the inner *animus* of each woman. Not only that we contain our opposites, but that we *are* our opposites. This really is a celebration of the complexity of life.

The play between forms I call the Tao Dance. It is the *Way* of all beings to seek out each other and embrace that which is different from one's own being, only to find a striking bond of sameness within the other as the forms move together. On an intrapersonal level, this dance can be between the parts of the soul: conscious and unconscious. I am caught dancing with my shadow whenever I experience inner conflict or am pulled in several directions. Resolution comes if I dance long enough. Observing the movement itself, I often forget the conflict, and then somehow it takes care of itself while I learn some new steps with my partner. My favorite story about this is Jacob Wrestling with the Angel.

Alone in the desert and perhaps in grave conflict, Jacob's attention and energy were diverted from his problems by an intrusive spirit—perhaps the embodied other side of his conscious experience. The Angel wanted to dance, I believe, but Jacob wrestled. He fought and fought, and despite himself, the Angel taught him that even wrestling, done faithfully, can be a form of passionate embrace. Finally toward dawn the Angel asked Jacob to let go. He answered simply: "I will not let you go until you bless me." Blessing is what he wanted. Recognition. Acceptance. Soon blessing came out of the struggle. And Jacob limped a little for the rest of his life to remind him of what he learned that night.

For me, the white deer is perhaps an Angel. Certainly not because it is white, but because it is the opposite of what one expects, and so it is a teacher, a reminder. Beware of the lesson, it says. Do not turn your back on Angels. Take up the dance and learn the blessing. Most pain is the result of resistance. If I learn to stop struggling and to move with my partner—whatever or whoever that might be—something new can happen. I might be able to give what I didn't know I had. I might be blessed.

\* \* \*

In French, *blessé* means "wounded one." To be wounded is to be broken through, to be broken open by a powerful touch. Opposites play again, for to be wounded in blessing is to be made whole. To be touched by the powerful hands of Angels is to be opened and healed. Jacob may have become physically lame as a reminder of his holy encounter, but it was as a direct result of that encounter that his name was changed to Israel—one-who-struggles-with-God-and-prevails—and he became the wise founder and ruler of an entire nation. He learned that weakness is not the same as vulnerability. Invulnerability is weakness. His weakness had been in running away from his problems; had he run from the Angel, he would have been weak again.

Instead, he let the Angel touch him, touch him powerfully enough to open him, and the lameness was to show that he was forever changed by the encounter. He had been wounded-blessed. He had been blessed-wounded: blessed through his wound and wounded by his blessing. The change made him powerful. Had he been invulnerable and closed, his rigidity would have made him the victim of any wind that came along. The Tao Dance with the Angel taught him to bend and yield and keep moving until he learned to move *with* the other.

Now not for nothing is the most powerful form of blessing given with the laying on of hands. Not for nothing is it a convention, when being blessed, to kneel. I cannot run away if I am kneeling. I am open to being touched. I may be touched so deeply and so powerfully that I am changed, and I may be changed so significantly that there is a visible difference in my form. It is a custom especially to bless people on their birthdays. A real birthday blessing is a wish for happiness: "May you be happy—may you be in harmony with what happens." But it is also more: "May this blessing give you the power to grow strong from your wounds."

I wonder why I have not seen the white deer. Perhaps it has been wounded or killed. Hunting season is not long over, and there are always evil people who love killing for its own sake, or to give themselves trophies of death. I do not think so. I think this deer is cunning. I think it appears in random moments to human eyes as a special blessing. Maybe I will see the deer nearer the time of my birthday, in spring.

*Why I Came to the Country, or Persephone Goes West*

> The whole venture
> is embarrassing.

Kissing my friends Goodbye
I mutter, "I wish I knew
what I was doing. . . ."

I have to go there.
I want to go there.
And I am loath to go.

The drive across mountains,
through deserts, finally
following the River home.

A naked season.
All the tree-bones exposed.
Browned Earth. Underground
pipes burst; aerial antenna bent,
toolshed blown down
in the Christmas storm.
Garbage strewn about.
The gate to the field wide open.

This is what
greets me.

I want to tear up
the grape vines that last summer choked my cherry trees,
I want to grab their dry tendrils
and send them packing.
I want to cut down the pampas grass
before it comes to the door demanding meat.
I want to plant roses—lots of them.

Instead, I leave the debris
for the insurance man,
scoop up armloads of rotten leaves
from the porch into plastic bags,

rake out the pond, wash windows
between storms, ponder futility
in all forms, bake muffins to keep warm,
keep the stewpot going for hearty smells,
count cars on the gravel road,
order new curtains,
visit the neighbors,
drink gallons of tea,
stay in bed,
listen to the wind,
think I hear wolves
howling at night,
find my own grief,
begin to feel it fully,
keep my skin wet,
let red sweat drop
on the paper,
and wait wait wait
for something new to happen.

*Six*
# Humus

Sunday morning. Listen to "House Blend" from Portland's public radio. Wash hair. Dry it by dancing to Baroque music and George Winston's wonderful lilting piano version of Pachelbel's Canon in D. Dance to the opening tulips and bright irises that came in your Valentine bouquet. Dance to the rain. No mountain today. A rain day. Give the violets a drink. Have breakfast: blueberry waffles with marmalade and tea. Give thanks. Remember why you are here.

I am here to let nature nurture me.

I am here to listen to the heartbeat of Mother Earth.

I am here to worship and dream.

I am here to remember my origin.

I come from the earth. She is my mother. Her bones are my bones and my bones will become hers again.

I am human. That means that I am humus. My body is the same as earth's body. I am nature. I am animal, animated, spirited.

When we forget that we are humus, we are disembodied and dispirited. Life has its ways of calling us back. If we are recalcitrant, we may be humiliated, which is to have our noses rubbed in the earth. If we are receptive, we may be taken up in awe and be moved by beauty or renewed kinship to our knees in sheer trembling joy—we may be humbled, which is to remember who we are with such gratitude that we want to kiss the earth.

There are moments every day when I am reminded and humbled and given anew the joy of true gratitude: when I bathe my body and see the fine hairs on naked skin which once long ago was covered with protective fur, when I needed more warmth to sustain the ice ages of earth; and when I eat, I am reminded that we are all part of the food chain. What I eat is part of creation as I am. I thank the beautiful animal and vegetable creatures for giving their lives that I might live. Their bodies will become my strength to work and play. One day my body will return to our mother and be food for them. My body will be their strength then, will help them to move through the dark and lift their faces to the sun.

I love being a creature. I love not being God, but God's child. I love having inherited creativity from my Creator.

I love being able to laugh. I wonder if some of the strange sounds we hear from horses and dogs and sheep and cows and cats are their own laughter. I hope so. To laugh, to be totally limp with hilarity, is an instant relaxation exercise. We would be relieved of stress if we spent a large portion of each day laughing—I mean doubled-over, whole-hearted, beside-oneself laughter. When we are doubled-over in pure pleasure, in the sweet spasm of laughter, our eyes are focused on the earth, and as we experience this great pleasure of laughter and its power to loosen us, it is humor that shows us humans the humus from which everything comes.

When I think of laughter in general, I think of my grandmother. She was a great laugher. She sat in her rocking chair and I sat in mine in her little house under the fir trees, and we would tell stories and trade jokes and talk silly and keep those chairs going with our belly laughs for hours and hours. The time I spent with her was my best growing time. She raised me on laughter. That was her bounty.

Her son, my father, was a good laugher, too. It was he who taught me to play. Children may know how to play naturally but play needs encouragement. It can be scared out of us, one way or another. My father showed me that some of the best things in life come from plain fun. I think that work is activity with purpose, and play is activity for its own sake, for the pleasure of itself. What begins the latter and keeps it going is often curiosity: one thing leads to another and another, and often what began in curiosity burgeons in discovery and billows out into new creation. Most creativity is accidental, the sweet serendipity of expecting one thing and finding another that is even better, and it comes from the curious enterprise of simply poking around.

All of this is earthy business. There is not much difference between making mud pies and clay statues, sand castles or blown glass, snowpeople or marble sculptures. The difference is only in the duration: someone played with mud long enough to find clay.

One of the best things about music is that it doesn't pretend not to be play. It openly says, Listen! I'm going to play for you. Or an elegant instrument challenges a human being: Play me!

Earth makes some of the best music all by herself. Her rivers and waterfalls, streams and oceans make astonishingly beautiful symphonies. The thunder in her clouds can waken with a Big Band drum roll. And what about the sweet percussion of rain on rock, the string variations of wind through leaves? All free entertainment for anyone who takes time to listen, marvel, and enjoy. Humbling. My own human voice, after all, is part of this. And every musical instrument of human creation comes from the same earth materials of metal or wood that originally sang in clear chorus in the wild. Even skin has sound. And the human body is not shaped too differently from that of a cello. . . .

It all comes to the mystery of the body. The earth's body, and every individual body born on the earth, every energy that finds home in some form. Our bodies are all essential parts and functions of the earth's body, as the mitochondria, originally separate animal forms, are now incorporated in our cells as essential parts of our bodies. And the earth's body is part of the body of the star we call Sun, our grandmother, and her body is part of the larger galaxy, which is part of the body of the universe, all of which is part of the body of God who gave birth to us in the Beginning. . . . Perhaps the body of God is sheer energy, and that energy longed for form so intensely that Light was born, and Light longed for Variety so intensely that darkness and number and color came tumbling into being, and the Mother of All said, "This is good. Now we will play."

Our play is bittersweet because each form as we know it ends. Variety is possible so far as we know only within a rhythm of limitation and return. This is what may be called the Divine Economy. Nothing is wasted. Forms die only to change into new forms and return. When one form has grown to meet its own limitation, it yields to transformation in a breathless meeting with new forms. We call this death. We call it an end because we don't yet understand it. But it is as truly part of life as darkness is of light: the essence, the inside, the secret unknowable kernel of the seed, the hidden yolk of the egg. The seed rots and new green pushes through. The egg breaks and a new form spills out.

When my mother died, I presided at her body's burial. As I uttered the ancient prayers, a realization broke through into my consciousness. I was returning my mother's body to Mother Earth, planting the seed of her new body from my point of view, because I assume that she already was in her new body, but this act of burial was for my benefit. It was as if I had before me a fully mature, majestic pine tree, and beside it a small, shriveled seed, and someone from another planet who had no knowledge of earth botany asked me what these two things were, and I answered, "They are the same thing. This is the seed which will die and break open and grow into this tree." The extraterrestrial would be completely bewildered, having no experience and no frame of reference for my story. But from my own experience, I knew it to be true, even commonplace. So we are from another world than the world on the other side of what we see in time as death. We have no frame of reference, no way to understand. We can only imagine and say "It is *as if.* . . ." We can only play with the possibilities. Meanwhile, we have our own grief at change and separation to endure, and the earth comforts us. Nature nurtures itself: flowers and trees and waters and the solid ground beneath our feet, and mind-opening sunsets and sunrises before our eyes, these say to us: You belong here now. We are all of the same body. The promise of what follows can only grow out of this in glory, as the tree from the seed. . . .

I buried my oldest friend last fall. She was ninety-two years old. We played her piano together every Tuesday afternoon for five years. She was a retired physician, a healing woman, and after music, we sat in her bright kitchen with tea and told stories and laughed. Her name was Alice, the same as my grandmother's. When Alice died, it was my privilege to return her body to the earth. The form that was her body had been cremated, further transformed by fire. I had scattered ashes on the earth and in water before, but Alice's ashes were to be be buried all in one place near the rest of her family. I held the box that contained the body that had contained her life. I held her bones as one would hold a baby. Whatever it is that happens in death, or what we (in our inexperience) call death, we are surely newborn. For the first time as a priest, I literally went into the grave with someone, because in order to lower the small box into the urn at the bottom of a hole in the ground, I had to kneel down on my belly and reach deep. Phil (my loving priest-husband and Alice's great-nephew) held me up by my stole, which functioned as a life-line, and I reached all the way inside Mother Earth's skin to return a daughter to her. I was a midwife in reverse, helping to return the gift, child back to mother, earth back to earth, and bone back to stone. Then I lowered the heavy gilded iron lid on my friend's life, with some russet and gold autumn leaves, and whispered, "Goodbye, Dearheart," to the part of her that I had known.

A few days later, I drove with Phil to my father's family cemetery in Henry, Illinois, to return some of his ashes there. He had died nearly a year earlier, but my pilgrimage of burial rites had been interrupted by winter and by many miles' distance between burial places. It was important to me to honor my father's life by returning his body to the several places important to him, and I judged their importance in relationship to his own creative bonds.

First, I gave a portion of the ashes of his body back to the particular humus beneath a fig tree which he had planted thirty years before on the grounds of his first church in Oregon, which he himself started as a young priest. The tree was thriving these years later; its fruit flourished. Now my father's body, which helped initially to encourage the tree's life, would feed and nourish it even more directly in its mature years. I returned ash to earth, and death to life.

Later, in the summer, I went with Papa's friend to a sequoia tree they had planted together, near another church where he had ministered for many years. I poured out the beautiful white ash and bone chips that looked like broken sea shells at the base of that tree, and with our four hands, daughter and friend covered the gift with new earth. Nothing is wasted. From remains, nutrients will flow right into the roots of that regal creature. There I uttered a child's prayer: "I bless these bones from which I come, and give them back to Earth, our home."

At the fig tree, my own friend Pesha helped me with her daughter Valerie, who was my father's Godchild, and whose own son Michael I had recently baptized. Now at the sequoia tree, my father's friend had done the digging, and as we stood up and looked at the other flora growing nearby, he said "Your father and I planted those irises, too. Let me dig one up for you to plant in your new garden." I survived my transplant home, and so did the iris. It is yellow. It came up like the sun itself two summers after planting, right in the middle of a group of daffodils whose buried bulbs I couldn't see at the time of planting!

I bless and water the humus and mingle my own skin cells and sweat into the topsoil of earth's skin, and take deep comfort. The iris is named for the Goddess Iris, in charge of rainbows and good news. I am getting the message, which is indeed good news, that we are all part of each other, not symbolically, but completely— interparticipatory relatives. Even as our bodies decompose we continue to compose the life of a larger body, and are part of a history larger and more ancient than our own. We are all ancestors.

I am not here just to tend the earth. Earth tends me.

### Mater

Mater (Mother)
materia
of Earth, *we—*
*matter.*

Sinews,
bone, the many
molecules
shudder

in leaving
as in loving.

So do not put
those thoroughly
changed ones
into the cold
past tense too soon,
saying, "We loved her,"
or "How good he was."

We continue to be
and belong,
and the love also

goes on—forever
and ever.

*We matter.*


## Ancestors

Three months back
the dining room closed
in the Henry Hotel.
We went to the Marina,
famous for catfish
from the Illinois River.

A glistening autumn day,
morning through scarlet
farms and orange fields,
amber oak trees on land
homesteaded by my great-
grandfather.

I came to bury you, Father,
carried your ashes across
three states in a clear
mason jar to lay your bones
in the bosom of your ancestors.

None of our Williamses
in the Henry Cemetery.
Where are they? Caretaker
sent us west to old
Sugargrove Graveyard.
Your son-in-law devotedly
climbed the locked wrought

iron gate and sought our kin
on the tree-shaded hill,
part of a farm now.
Not here either.

Finally, Mrs. Caretaker
called out, "I know where
your family is!
All the Williamses are up
in Putnam County Cemetery."

There was the half-ton meteorite
that made a hole halfway to Japan
in Uncle Irwin's front yard
in 1880—and to the right
in a bright sun orb,
little Comfort Hope,
born and died
the same winter day that year.

Near the neatly raked gravel road
I found your mother, Alice Delphine
Williams, and her mother and father,
Alice Little and George Williams.

Grandma was born in 1897,
the year her father died.
Great-grandfather—"Papa"
in her stories—was a big
gentle man, constable
in Putnam County, spent some
time in jail for accidentally
shooting an escaped convict
to death, stepped on a rusty nail
in the stable and left Grandma
an orphaned baby.

His widow gave up teaching others'
children and made her living
as midwife—trudged waisthigh
through snow, a tiny amazon,
to deliver babies in Tiskilwa.

Aunt Melinda Morgan watched her
four young until her madness
made her a danger to them.
She wanted to keep the baby
for her own, saying, "That's my child,
I brought that child from Connecticut!"

I stand among their graves,
these brave ones I never knew,
my old ones, heroes of my humbling
history, these plain people.
I pour my father's ash
over his mother's heart
near his grandparents' grave:
"Make Your face to shine upon him
and be gracious unto him . . ."
then dust the oldest stone
in our section, Frances Williams,
died September 1843, aged sixty-one years.
I have a picture of Papa alive,
kneeling, leaning on her tombstone
almost casually, looking straight
and clear-eyed into the camera.
He was fifty-eight.

I take my own thirty-six years in my hands and place
the last white chips
around and on top
of the meteorite in the center.
We *are* starstuff. . . . Be a star.

"Lift up the light of Your countenance
upon him and give him peace."
What a privilege to be born,
to be human, to be part of this.
I bless our ancestors for my life
and days, kiss the bone on ancient stone
and turn for home.

                    October 14, 1983
                    My mother's seventy-fourth birthday
                    by the old Russian (Julian) calendar


## Family Reunion

Six million years since
Grandma and Grandpa Bacteria
hatched up the possibility
of the rest of us.

Now, chestnut, sandpiper, turtle,
eagle, human, lily, mushroom
and horse have climbed out
of the crack in our cosmic egg,
riding the Great Light.

We are more complicated,
to be sure, more long-lived,
more opinionated and fragile—
but not more creative,
extravagant, or efficient
than our great-grandparents,
those one-celled creatures
that still live in our midst,

that still have the power
to give us life
and also to kill,

to whom we owe
our power to breathe
and birth and laugh,
write plays, wage sports,
learn peace, or kill
ourselves.

*Seven*
# The Salmon

Dawn-rose. Angel Mountain appears after a week's absence from vision. I remember the Christmas hymn, "Break forth, O beauteous heavenly light, and usher in the morning. . . ." Gentle wings of pink light unfurl from the central image of radiant white. My eye, seldom awake so early, is unaccustomed to the colors of change in the eastern sky. I bless the transition from night to day. I reflect and rejoice in this second Sunday morning surprise. The Creator's softest colors shine in the radiant rose of divine mother-love. I revel and lean into the light. I receive the maternal embrace of this live volcano in the hours of her peace. She is the white bosom filled with nutrients that surge up to the surface of the earth from the mantle and core far below. Creatures that suckle near ocean volcanoes have the richest blood in the sea: the giant tube worms and red-blooded clams that live far down around the flowing vents on the Pacific Ridge. Hungrily I take in rich vitamins for the eye—a contented land-creature, and fed on light, I grow.

This Valentine's Day was Oregon's 125th birthday as a state. Mt. Hood came out to celebrate, a Big White Valentine. I felt gratitude myself for having been made in this state. It is a place where the creation process is busiest on earth. The Pacific Oceanic Plate continues to push under the continent, and the rumbling responses of the continental crust shake and shudder under emerging mountain ranges. We surface creatures carry on our lives in the constant aftershocks of earth quaking into new forms. I am a child of all this. And I want to exercise my birthright to be an active participant.

After fifteen years away, I have come home. So many chain-reacting circumstances took and kept me away. I felt like a landlocked fish, the particular fish of this part of the world—the salmon.

The salmon is spawned in high mountain streams nestled in the cloud-touching peaks of the Cascades. Nurtured on mountain-nutrients for a year, the young fish begins its free-fall descent downriver to the sea. There it thrives, exploring the wide world of water where all life began, the original womb of the earth, now opened for travel. The adventurer moves freely through space and time, until its own time for return. Then all instincts converge and alert the creature to turn itself toward home and find its way back to the source or die trying. Then the fish itself changes color, marking its own time of transition. It becomes sunset red.

More treacherous than the ride seaward, the journey home is all upstream, against the current, of necessity.

The creative fulfillment of this climb by each solitary fish is its only chance to mate and take its part in the onward flow of life. Without the elaborate production of the Great Climb Home, no fish can enjoy the orgasmic reproduction rite for which it was born.

As the new color of its body deepens, the fish's face curls into a distinctive gnarl, the jaws so twisted that it will not be able to eat again. Each day of its quest the fish grows weaker, and its tasks become more challenging: to leap the length of increasingly steep waterfalls; to evade the grasp of hungry bears; to stay on course. The salmon finds its way to the mouth of its own river most likely by instinctively remembering its own stars. The eye again leads. How the stars were placed in the sky in relationship to one's own beginnings . . . a new way of viewing astrology!

Now the only help comes from within, in the sheer will to continue and bring to completion the salmon's own life force. When external aid is offered, it may cause stark terror until, again, necessity intervenes and makes a pathway clear. Artificially constructed fish ladders are humanity's attempt to help, but the unnatural sharp metal angles and closed tunnels of the ladders cannot be welcoming. What the fish are saved in energy they may lose in fear. If they succeeded in swimming through what the good will of others has set in their way, they have yet to find strength for the last and hardest challenge.

Once the fish come to their own native lake, they have to choose a mate, and make their way through the shallow rockbeds to the highest part of the small finger lakes to spawn their own offspring. Many will be beached on the way, become confused and lost in too-shallow water and die breathlessly on the dangerous dry shore. The mate may delay too long in trying to revive its partner, and go the same way. Those with strength and sound instincts that live through this final course of the journey come to a nesting place at the end. This is where they were born, and this is where they will mate, give birth, and die.

The fish distorts its battered body further by using it as a shovel to dig its nest. Only two creatures drawn to a shared purpose could be so attractive to each other after all these physical ravages, but the fish proceed with their bio-dance, and for a few days transcend their pain in a sexual orgy. Their children (bred in a last burst of sexual energy) are spawned, and their challenge begins immediately, for many eggs will become breakfast for other creatures before their own lives break out of the shell. Meanwhile, the exhausted parents curl themselves together and wait for death.

My homecoming totem is indeed the salmon. I am led to the mouth of my river from friendly exile in my inland sea, and I reverse the salmon's journey, approaching my mountains from the east. My move toward rebirth is westward, while their sunset bodies climb through water in the direction of dawn. I do not know what challenges await me, but I know I must follow my stars to find out. I do not know if I will have strength for the journey, but I know I must use all I have to come to the place where I, too, can create, or something in me will die.

As the salmon's body becomes a deeper color and light shines against it with an intensity that blinds other creatures and keeps the fish from becoming their dinner, I, too, pray for help and protection, within and without, on my way.

I asked my friends to pray for me on my journey before I set out last fall. One of them responded, "What shall I pray?"

"Pray that I may have the courage to live truthfully."

Now I am here, nestled at the foot of the Mountain, climbing my way to her heart through my eyes. I begin to feel movement within me. I look west, to the sea, and feel an ocean surge in my breast. I do not know what will swim forth from my mind, but I watch light playing on the colors around and within me, and I am willing to wait in grateful ecstasy.

### Piscean Moon

Salmon gleam
rose red one mile
far and deep at sea—
seagulls glimmer
silvershimmer on
sleeping rocks
near shore—
beyond shining
amethyst sand
a fiery apricot
full moon resting
on black water.

## Chinook

So near my goal
an imponderable weight
presses down, stresses
and shapes to deform.
My tortured body
twists into the current
and now ten million tons
of water come down
upon me, all heavy,
all is heavy, all slowed
to an imponderable wait
so near to home.
Did you bring me over
the threshold to die?


## Homecoming

Those fish are not the only
animals driven home by death.

I too have been at sea,
a deep sea swimmer.

I too have grown
red-fleshed and thin-

blooded
in my journey.

An inland ocean's holding,
submerged in duty, learning,

diving off the edge of inner
ridges unrelenting and on fire,

seeing miracles
at the Source.

I too know my inkling times
and their span.

Eons verge symmetrically.
In no time, the time of Return.

At first no hint
of failing,

the waning breath
and defiant

leap
of two-thirds free.

All changed.
Time burned out of me.

Silver-skinned,
half turned to salt,

I start the end,
all atoms urging.

The Dance begins.
We turn and turn again

in unison,
bones and happy molecules

and the compact
organs singing:

Out of the depths
to the rivers, and light.

I am coming
to the hard and gentle place

for the Great Marriage
to propagate my kind.

I am becoming
the river and light

in my longing.
I am metamorphic,

a living seaplane
in my dreams,

fins unfolding
into wings.

I am a living
seaflower

climbing rivermountains
impossibly.

My labor toward death
is Original Play.

I remember this
struggle

is how I was born,
came to be.

My scaly petals cover, kiss
my sisters' eggs in passing.

My pink blood blesses, greets
tomorrow, fades gratefully

into another body.


## Salmon Return

Do not plant me
in too-high lakes
and leave me to die,

climbing against the current
never to take nourishment
again, damaged by men's nets,
determined, determined
to go home.

I risk all,
lose all.

From too-shallow basins
I fly up waterwalls,
become breakfast for bears,
foxes, seagulls, my children
magpies' supper,

am pushed through false tunnels
up metal ladders, frightened
all the way.

Survive. Survive.

Five years at sea,
then I track my way
through the impossible,
journey to thrive
in a few hours ecstasy
when I live only to love,
then die with my mate
content in five days.

My body transforms for this,
red and round with roe,
my face an obsessive mask,
teeth tortured upward
with one purpose under stars:
home. Home.

In my final waters
at the top of the world
my faithful mate and I
prepare to dance and die.

Together we rise along rocks,
ripe for love, past beached
friends too weak for this orgy
of fulfilling glory.

Now the last brief fall up,
my life-battered body too weary
for this small step at the end.

My children! My love!
Bring me home!
Strength for this journey!
Oh! breath still in me,
let me leap!

*Eight*
# The Well

This is my happy birthday house. I set my sights on it for the first time two years ago. It was the beginning of miracles.

After my talk at Stanford University, I was to meet Phil in Oregon for our winter vacation together. I flew north from California and he flew west from Minnesota. Alone on my flight, with the full moon visible out my window and over my right shoulder, I prayed to be released from my own psychological blocks against moving back to Oregon, because I knew that it was past time that I needed to do that. I had been away from my Source for thirteen years and my blood was beginning to curdle.

The blocks existed because I had reason to believe that my own tradition—the Episcopal Church—would not welcome me back as a woman priest. Even though I had been the first woman to be ordained a deacon here, my controversial ordination to the priesthood three years later was another matter. But that was eight years before, and, as they say, water under the bridge. So it was time for me to let go of my fear, time to cross my bridge.

I had been practicing letting go of fear for some time. That night I must have let it leave me all at once, at least for that part of my journey. I had discovered the purpose of fear, and I had allowed it to serve me, for a change. And the change for which it served me was about to happen! My idea about fear is that it is a natural tool for survival, intrinsic in creation. Human beings, however, having lost sight of it as a tool, have come to misuse it as a deterrent. Consider that fear is a Stop sign. The proper way to treat a Stop sign is to heed its suggestion and stop, then attend to the situation by looking and listening in all directions, basing the decision to move forward in the direction of choice on the information gleaned by our attention. We may move straight ahead or turn. Or we may see that we are off course, and turn around. The sign offers us the opportunity to make a free choice based on accurate information, by making use of all our discretionary senses and our ability to discern the presence or absence of danger, then decide which action and timing are most appropriate.

I was ready to come home. The sign was where it belonged. It was I who had gone off the road. What better place than the open sky, finding myself parallel to the night-lantern moon, for my mind to open? I realized my own participation in my exile myth that had kept me for years from having what I wanted, and now seriously needed. I had cast people whom I didn't even know as ogres and myself as victim in my exile myth: *They* won't like it if I come back here. I had already discovered that the myth was a lie and made positive human contact with the very people I had feared. What remained to be dispelled was any residue of doubt in my own mind that I deserved to be happy. Once this residue is gone, however, what remains is the hard work of achieving happiness—a skill which requires steady practice. I rolled up my sleeves by consulting the *I Ching* again, to see what my unconscious and divine Grace were up to.

Still in the air and out in the dark of that night sky of mystery, solitude, and an array of luminous company far away, I received two oracles: *The Well*, and *Keeping Still, The Mountain*.

The symbolic nature of the *I Ching* oracles is sacrosanct. I consider it an expression of the divine humor of our Creator that in this case, lest my density interfere with destiny, I was to get the message in living color the next day.

Now the spiritual meaning represented in the oracle, *The Well*, is this: Go down to the very foundations of life and attend to the deepest, innermost needs. What is gained on a personal level will overflow into the common good in the form of lasting spiritual values that will enhance humanity. The setting may change, but the source of life does not change. Though the water is given, human carelessness may break the jug and cause the disaster of waste. In order to receive the full good of the gift, all the parts must cooperate for the benefit of the whole. And in my case that night, the message evolved into the next, *Keeping Still, The Mountain*, whose meaning is this: Achieve a quiet heart by discerning the appropriate times for keeping still and for moving forward. Light comes into life from the balance of rest and movement in harmony with the demands of the time. Harmony signifies the end and the beginning of all movement. When one has come to true peace of mind, one understands and works with the universal laws of nature flowing from the Great Harmony, and what is known in the soul freely turns to the outside world for the good of all. It is wise not to allow one's thoughts to go beyond the situation but first to discern the nature of the movement, and then respond in harmony with the deepest levels of awareness, lest the heart become sore and weary in working on what cannot yet be known.

Very sound advice, I thought.

As always, I expected the good counsel of the inner heart to remain on a subtle and inner plane. But I was flying into the realm of live volcanoes, after all: foolish expectation!

The next day was one of those breathtaking crystalline days when the mountains radiate like cut diamonds in an azure setting. Phil and I knew we had better seize the day indeed, for such opportunities come rarely in the winter. We went mountain-watching.

By instinct I guided us down the road with the best mountain views. I knew when not to follow it off to the prominent left but to veer to the right another mile

until we were ordered by a large arrow to turn sharply
to the right, and I also knew by sure instinct that this
was the moment to disregard the sign and boldly to
turn left in the opposite direction right in front of it. I
explained to Phil, "I saw the sunset on the Mountain
from here two years ago and I'd forgotten all about it
until now. I thought then how wonderful it would be
to live here someday."

At that moment, our eyes fell on the "For Sale" sign
in front of the house, and the elderly woman and man
who had built the house were standing in the driveway
smiling with their arms outstretched to us in welcome.
The outside of the house did nothing for me, but the
moment I stepped inside, I recognized the house to be
mine, waiting for me to come home to it. How or when
I had no idea. From every window and door on the
crucial east-facing side, the Mountain reigned. And on
the west, sunset over a great raspberry field. On the
Mountainside were also sloping meadows feeding sheep
and horses and even grazing grey geese and goats, and
a golden knoll on the north flank to serve as a bowl for
gloaming light, with a fir-covered ridge on the south
that sheltered a family of eagles, probably bears, once a
mountain lion, and always, deer. This was where I
belonged. In case I doubted, due to the external fact of
having no means at the moment of buying the house
and its nearly two acres, there was a ninety-foot *Well*
in the front yard, and, of course, *The Mountain,
Keeping Still*, in the backyard. Skeptic that I am, I was
too smitten to resist. I laughed in tacit agreement with
what appeared to be my Creator's idea for my destiny,

though I had no idea how it would be accomplished.

Then, nine months from the time that we had first seen the House, my father died.

I had not seen my father in four months, since we happened to share vacation time with him in Oregon that June. He had just come back from a splendid month in England and France. Through a quirk of Northwest Airlines, we were blessed with another miracle when his flight was re-routed to stop for customs in Minneapolis instead of Denver before his final destination in southern California. We spent time well together for those final minutes between planes, looking at maps while he told stories and named the places of his journey.

It was not an ordinary trip, but a special pilgrimage "In the Footsteps of Thomas à Becket," involving a candlelight meditation in Canterbury Cathedral and a visit with the Archbishop of Canterbury. The next day the group took a bus trip in the rain along the route of Becket's exile in northern France. The driver became desperately lost and my father saved the day by leading the whole company of travelers in song for four hours while they found their way.

It was the first time in twenty years he had traveled alone, and it was a *tour de force* for him to be able to make new friends and be his own person after so many years of isolation when his health kept him a prisoner from life. Now I saw him radiant and robust, triumphant, fully alive. Those years of illness in which he had feared death and so kept himself from life were over, and indeed now that he had come alive, it was all right, in the truest sense, for him to die. He had grown into readiness for the Larger Life.

I must have sensed this on some level when Phil and I walked away from him at the airport and turned to see him smile and wave. He looked serene, as I had seen him only as a young man, and I wanted to run back and tell him how proud of him I was. Phil said, "There will be another time, Honey. We're late for the meeting we're going to." I agreed, but something in me regretted not following my inclination. Since my first experiences with death I have vowed never to hold back words of praise or love, but that time I did, yielding to the conflicting need for us to be somewhere else with other people who were waiting for us.

The next night I wanted to call California to ask if my father had arrived safely and was rested. He had come through Minnesota during the first snow of the season. I waited, thinking to give him an extra day. That second night, he died peacefully in his sleep, having achieved a full life.

I flew to the California lower desert the next morning, and on my father's nightstand, I found the advance copy of my book, *Life is Goodbye/Life is Hello*, which I'd sent him while he was away. It was always his custom to read a book straight through before going to sleep at night. I knew that reading the book I had inscribed "To my father, in deep gratitude for all you have given, all you have taught me," was the last thing he did before he went to sleep and woke up with God. It was like a kiss from heaven.

The rest of that fall and winter I was occupied tending to his business and doing my own grief work.

The dream of living in Oregon seemed to be slipping away. The financial means to make the necessary job possible were being siphoned elsewhere. Perhaps not ultimately, but at least in the mortal sphere—as we see in the possibilities we have created for self-destruction— human beings have the terrible power to thwart the Great Harmony.

In February, a year since we had found the House, the owners called to tell us that they could no longer hold it for us in faith that a breakthrough would let us buy it. I told them I understood and asked only that if someone made an offer, they let us know "in case a miracle happens" so that we could buy it after all. They were sad because they had been praying for us and they felt that their house was meant to be ours. We were sad, too. After the conversation I cried and prayed, "Into your hands I commend our house." I thought that that was the end of it. But three days later I got another call from Oregon, this time from my father's attorney who had never called me before. He said, "This morning we found a document in your father's file which we'd forgotten about and which has been virtually lost for eight years. It seems that you have a bit more in your inheritance than we knew." I bought my dream house.

It was on my birthday, May 15, that I signed the closing papers. It was my father's last birthday present to me. Instead of the flowers which he usually gave me, he had given me a whole garden with a house in the middle. Surrounded by flowers and fruit trees, a place to create a new home and a new life had been given into my hands.

My inheritance came to mean more than money with which to invest in a future, though it was predominantly just that. My inheritance was the fulfillment of my birthright, to become my own person. My father had achieved true independence in the last year of his life, since his health had improved through his own intensive treatment program, even though his heart had endured too much over the years of sickness to give him a future. Now he extended to me, in his death, the gift of independence and a future in which to experience it in the place I had chosen. He gave me the way home.

Not that I am no longer limited, but that I am able to transcend my limitation to a degree not possible before, by becoming an independently propertied woman. The main achievement was to do this without guilt. And Phil celebrated this gift with me, himself mature man enough to enjoy not being burdened by my need for his income. And I am practicing being mature woman enough to enjoy my inheritance and the independence it gives me. My father gave me life twice: in my birth as a child, and in my rebirth as an adult. And my mother also shares in the gift, since it was my inheritance from her and the sale of her house that enabled us to buy our Minnesota home, which will ultimately in its resale complete the purchase of the Oregon property.

I am allowing the vision to unfold. It is creating itself. It is my vision, but my commitment is to serve it and to help it into being, which I do primarily by trusting in the future. I still do not know the way, but I am indeed open to the way, for it has been steadfast in its opening to me so far.

The theme of my house is transfiguration. It came to me by way of its symbol, the peacock. Peacocks appear in the fiction of Flannery O'Connor as a symbol of the Transfiguration of Christ—the manifestation of inner radiance which Peter, James, and John witnessed on Mt. Tabor. One of the old volcanoes in Portland is named Mt. Tabor. Transfiguration is illumination from within which brings with it deep transformation. In the Gospel narrative the most significant sentence of the story is, "A change came over him."

The story I am telling is not fiction. I could never get away with such corny coincidences in fiction. It is too wild not to be true. A change has come over me, too. A letting go of fear. An acceptance of gifts despite my old inclinations to demur. A willingness to act on a faith in the future, even when I do not feel confident. A determination to keep moving through my fear, to keep using the Stop sign in the right way by discerning, deciding, and acting. Some of my decisions may be very painful, requiring still more hard Goodbyes before the happy Hellos can happen. I want to stay faithful, because to thwart the Great Harmony is to sunder the future and bring harm.

I surround myself with icons of illumination and transformation. On the windows are peacock lace curtains. In the hallway on my father's French writing desk is a rosewood music box with a peacock and butterflies in gold-pink tones which Phil give me for Christmas. In the living room are a sofa and loveseat discovered by my sharp-eyed mother-by-marriage, Betty, who went on the first shopping expedition with me. These pieces of furniture bear soft-toned peacocks and are surrounded by garlands of lavender, blue, and gold roses that match my mother's pastel roses in their gold frame, the first piece to go inside the house as a token of her blessing. On the round walnut table is a bowl from India with a peacock in rose tones inside. And on the back of a mirror, two peacocks to show me what can become of the inner self, for when the bird lifts its tail in a sudden profusion of bright color— emerald and sapphire and brown with a shimmer of gold—it is no longer the obnoxious-sounding nuisance of its ordinary pose, but a creature whose main feature is *eyes*. These eyes do not see outward, for they merely decorate the animal's tail feathers. Rather, the thousand eyes that the bird trails behind it mirror, to those who witness the display, the possibility for radiance and luminosity that comes with the willingness to change for the better, to risk becoming more fully alive, to give inner potential for harmony a chance by *seeing* reality in new ways. A deep, true change of perspective is what is called for. Nothing I have seen is more harmonious or seemingly magical than the spread tail of the peacock, which is utterly common to the creature itself. What one naturally is can be glorious if one dares to show it, or is not too self-conscious to show it casually.

This house is now Wisdom House, the creation and extension of my own ministry, a center for spirituality— creativity and healing. At the first worship service in the chapel, it happened that the appointed scripture readings were for the Feast of the Transfiguration, beginning with the story of Moses's sojourn and receiving of the Law on that lively volcano, Mt. Sinai. The fire leapt with thunder and flame from within the mountain of God! And the prophet stayed there faithfully for forty days. Later, Yeshua (Jesus) was alone with his friends on Mt. Tabor when his body was transfigured in a powerful light and his friends were dismayed, and soon after he went into the wilderness to prepare for the challenge of the future for forty days by himself.

On the wall over the altar here is a present from my geologist Goddaughter, Holly, on the same birthday as my happy birthday house. It is a photograph of the burning crater of Mt. St. Helens, the only picture I have seen that shows the heart of the mountain on fire, its orange dome further illuminated by the light of the full moon. I am here with my own volcanos, attempting to be faithful.

There is a stone bench outside the house near the well in the front yard. The old artist who crafted this place inlaid rose quartz patterns in the stone with petrified wood. I sit here in well-being and consider the two wagon wheels he inserted in brick in the weathered wood fence. One wheel is under the Ponderosa pine, the other beneath the dogwood tree, with the young sweetgum between them. In front, the white heather is already in bloom, pollinated by insomniac bees in January. The wagon wheels remind me of the song, "All My Life's a Circle." This house is just two miles from where I lived nearly twenty years ago. They also remind me that life is at its best when in tandem:

partnerships make the most satisfying enterprises on life's voyage, especially when adventures lead to happy harbors for rest and celebration. And finally the wheels remind me of the pioneers who made impossible journeys over seas and across two treacherous mountain ranges to make new lives here. I can't complain, even if I don't always know where I'm going.

So when I turn off the main highway to get to Tapp Road and my Well, I wind down and down into the open valley through clusters of great and ancient Douglas fir trees, past the sapphire circle of Roslyn Lake, onto shadowy Coalman Road, past the moss-thick twin maples, across the white bridge over Cedar Creek full with snow-melt from high glaciers, and I ask, "Is this the road home?"

And for a few moments the question hovers and I hold my breath. Then the gratitude and gladness take hold of me in a twin embrace, as in the clearing before me in a sudden curve looms Angel Mountain.

Yes. This is the road home.

### Happy Birthday House

Here is my happy
birthday house,
dream house,
hello house,

here are my happy
hello flowers
and fountains
and fruits,

here are my happy
trees with their
spreading arms full
of green hellos,

here are my happy
honey bees and beetles
with their bright wings
humming, and

here are my birds
greeting the day
good morning.

Here are the horses
and sheep with their
children helloing,
and gardens with geese
greeting all, and

here, above all,
over all, with
rainbows arcing
across meadows
is my Angel Mountain,
white goddess rising
over rivers, laughing
volcano laughter
over valleys,
"Home! Hello! Hello!
Welcome home!"

*Nine*
# Open Hands

Go down to the very foundations of life. Attend to the deepest needs. Superficial changes alone will bring disaster. Observe the time for keeping still and listening.

I sweep leaves from around the well and watch the Mountain, keeping still. Tomorrow will be Ash Wednesday, when I will bless the neighbor women who will come to liturgy and, touching their hands with the dust of burned leaves, say to each one: "Remember, daughter of God, that you come from the earth and to the earth you shall return."

I remember that I am here with intention: my intention is to pay attention to the Great Mystery as it speaks in its thousand ways all around me.

To attend means several things. It means to serve. It means to wait. Waiting is the hardest work on earth. To wait on tables, to wait on the altar, to wait for birth, to wait at a deathbed, to submit to the tasks of patience, to become patient. To grow patient toward the human need for nurture and the divine need for nature. To honor the mutually intense needs between Creator and creature. To know that we spring from God's need for us, as our children spring from our need for them, as water springs from earth's need. To extend open hands toward need, at table and altar. At the altar of human need to open the hand of compassion, and at the table of divine need to open the hand of passionate praise. To give attention is to do so gladly. To stand at attention is to be ready for action. To *tend* is to care for, and to hold . . . tenderly.

Lent means "lengthening light." It is vital to remember this meaning. It is a time of rebirth in creation, time to attend to the many births around us, to keep still and to wait on the need-bed of things being born. Time to listen to things growing, breaking through the earth, lifting themselves to more light through longer days. Time to learn anew how to grow, break through, and lift ourselves toward the light. Keep still and learn.

Lent is a heart-braking time. Time to take our force away from the inner accelerator and give ourselves a brake. Time to stop driving and roll down the window and listen and smell the new air. I had a picnic on my patio this incredible afternoon, with black currant tea and Mozart's concerto for harp and flute blending perfectly with all the varied choruses outside, the bees and birds in ecstasy and riding the spring light in their singing flight. The season of longer light is often difficult when we forget how to lean and learn and shun stillness for noisy mortification. We learn little by maintaining control and making all the noise ourselves. The point is to let go a little to the wilderness rhythms within us.

Forty days in the wilderness. Nothing more. Nothing less.

What can be learned in forty days in the wilderness!

The time and place call for deep-down change. The transfiguration of the inner self. The opening and yielding of hidden places within. Time to let seeds fall. Time to prune trees and cut away the old excesses so the whole plant can grow more freely and truly. Time to gather leftover leaves from fall. Time to open up certain bulb roots and let them breathe. Time to bless and open the garden. To live leanly. To put down the fat that warmed us through winter and lighten up. To move more freely. To get outside . . . ourselves. *To look at the gifts of time*—this is how to *observe* a holy season.

Breathe. In and out. Fully. Open the inner senses. Receive and release. You are an essential part of the universe. You belong here. Receive and return the gift of life. Complete each breath. Do not put your foot down to intercept this immediate moment of grace. Stay awhile. Attend.

I came here in the fall, driving without human companionship through snow and fog across the Rocky Mountains and into the plains and desert. I was afraid of being caught in the snow, caught in the fog. I had the choice of staying where I was or moving through the elements. I chose then to move. And much to my amazement, the storm abated within a few miles and I was able to cross the steepest passes of the Rockies in bright sunlight that lit up the crimson, gold, and russet vermilion deciduous leaves like a rehearsal for Christmas.

The next morning came the thickest fog I-ever-didn't-see-through in Spokane, and I wondered if I should be sensible and let that stop me. But I listened to the locals, as I had in the Montana mini-blizzard, and took their confidence to heart. Ten miles later and, wondering if I would ever see the roadway again, I glanced at my watch for an eye-blink to look up and see for a hundred miles! I thought I'd imagined the fog, but a look in the rearview mirror confirmed where I'd been, as the desert spread out before me.

Later I followed the Columbia River to its mile-wide spill into the Pacific Ocean at Astoria, and south to the end of the Lewis and Clark Trail at Seaside and then my favorite place, Cannon Beach and Ecola Inn facing the great moss-and-lichen-coated monolith, Haystack Rock, a refuge for gulls. That day it was wind that dismayed me. One-hundred-mile-an-hour gales had slowed some, but still the wind could hold you up if you just rested on it, or knock you down if you didn't. There I watched an obsessive seagull a foot from my window trying to fly against the wind, flapping its heavy wings very, very slowly, its eyes blown shut, and not going anywhere. F l a p. . . . F F F L L L A A A P. . . . Finally, like a sensible bird, it paid attention to reality and stopped treading air, making itself a cozy shelter in sand to wait out the storm. The elements will have their way. Proceed or fall back, but *pay attention*.

In July when I moved into the house, I spent three weeks pulling weeds. After six weeks of rain since my predecessors had moved, I was surrounded by jungle. My first lesson from nature came when I pulled hard on a big tall weed and it slid out from its inch-deep rootbed. Then I gave a futile yank to a short critter that didn't budge. After some struggle on my part, and still no budge, I began to notice the ground ripple ten feet away; I pulled up a root that was three times the length of my own body. You have to admire creatures that anchor themselves like that. Not that the pattern was consistent. The point was that I never knew what resistance would answer me from the ground once I made contact with a weed. I practically had to be paid by my neighbors to go after the pretty white morning glory and purple fireweed. But pretty soon I was becoming ruthless, and out went the brassy Bellingham lilies as well. A flowerbed is no place for sentimentality.

My hands were mean and busy a good part of July, closed tight around their opposing powers in green. I was grateful to them as I took lessons in root-digging: when you start to go after something that is crowding out chosen life-forms, you may find yourself tracking convoluted tangles underground some distance away from where the thing showed itself. The source can be far from the sprout. Attend to the tangle and stay with the trail until the whole thing comes up, or your work will be to no avail. Then congratulate your failed opponent on its tenacity as you help it on its way toward the transforming powers of fire. Not unlike my work as a priest or gardener of the soul.

And not unlike the constant tending which the marriage garden requires. Toward the end of summer,

Phil came to help me clear the garden of overgrowth and re-fertilize it. It was a holy work we were doing together in our new garden, and it coincided with a time when we were doing just these same things in our marriage. Recognition of this inner and outer congruence gave us comfort.

A late fall and my return to Minnesota enabled me to excuse myself from yard work. When I came back at the end of January to begin my winter writing sabbatical in earnest, all the trees had let go of last year's leaves and their cast-off clothes were lying about rotting under my feet. Now I had to act.

Decked out in Minnesota earmuffs and down jacket I took rake in hand one forty-degree day—thinking it would probably not improve if I waited all winter—despite the accompanying forty-mile wind. But the wind didn't interfere too much because it was also raining at the time, and the leaves were too soggy to fly around out of hand. I struggled and sweated over the plastic leaf bags that only blew shut when I wanted them open and vice versa, abandoned my muffs and jacket on the wet grass, gave up trying to blow my nose and let it run in hope that no one would come just then for a social call. Triumphant, seconds before it started to pour and blow in earnest, I satisfied my own standards for a tidy lawn and let the naturally formed leaf piles under the bushes be, wishing them speedy transformation into mulch. The next day when the temperature bounced to unseasonal seventy and the sun lazed in a windless sky, I reconsidered these piles, and I wondered if my scratchy throat was perhaps a direct result of my impatient behavior of the day before.

It was then that I contracted to devise my own lesson from the leaves. If the trees could let go of them, so could I. I said to the remaining masses (which apparently had multiplied overnight), "I leave you dearly. Rot on where you are and make nice roses come May." I opened my grasp from around the red rake, relieved my hands of more uncomely blisters, and sat down to listen to the sun shine.

Now some months later, I wonder why the leaves are taking so long to become mulch. Every now and then I am tempted to help them along. But then I talk myself into being sensible. I need to distinguish between the time to work through a problem with both hands and the time to open my hands and sit back to watch my earthy partner do its own work. It is astonishingly difficult to keep my twitchy hands out of things, but I persist. Sitting back to watch the earth work gives me opportunity to reflect on the season and admire the capabilities of the rest of nature. Nature knows how to work on and redeem itself, by the grace of the Creator's hand and in its own creation. I am pleased and proud to be part of this, to do my part in support of earth's work as earth supports mine. It is the same work, really.

I think of the necessity of getting and staying out of my own way sometimes. Keeping my hands off the pile and letting it take its own time to become something useful, my own leaves turning themselves into mulch. I wonder if watching helps. The Creator watches over creation creating onward, and this surely gives life because it is the gift of ongoing love. So I watch my own processes, learning a loving detachment toward myself and others. Under an observing eye—my own—what needs to be changed in me is not worried and worked over, but allowed to become what the loving eye seeks. I remember when I was very young that my most effective teachers were those who said and interfered very little, but watched and waited on and for me as I struggled on my own to find the right word or the right number. I felt encouraged by their care and confidence in me, which was shown to me by their simple steadfast presence—silently, expectantly, watching, waiting. The power of the confident and caring eye. The teaching eye.

Now when I experience pain of any kind, or make myself unhappy with impatient response to frustration or delay, I step back from myself and become all eye. I observe how the negative feeling is halting or pushing my breath, and how my blocked breath is creating other sensations of pain in my body and spirit, and under my very detached and caring eye, my breath begins to change. The negative feeling dissolves. Quiet observation alone sometimes has this power. It calls one to attend to what one is doing, and what one wants to do, and quietly to dissolve the discord between the two.

Sometimes when I do not complete a breath, but take in too little or too much, or give back too little, there is a thought behind the thwarted act which says "The good in your life will leave you. Just take a little to make it last. Or take it all at once and hold on to it!" If I take a moment to hear this thought, I can speak to it and correct it as I correct my faulty breath. As I breathe in I say to my innermost self, "God loves me," and I take this in completely. As I return the love to the universe and breathe completely out, I affirm, "I am loving and loved." If I tighten my grip around my own throat in fear or frustration, I can intercept the negative pattern of blame and the breathless aim of accusation at myself or another by simply breathing forth, "Bless you. No blame."

Every morning here I wake up and say, "Thank you, God." When I open my eyes I see myself through the window-eyes of the house more truly than when I look in a mirror. I am this garden. I am learning my seasons along with its seasons.

It is a season to be blessed in being here. I hear my father's blessing coming to me as I look around this place with gratitude toward him. He regards me with a caring eye in the communion of saints, trusting me to make the most of the gift: "Create your own life. Live responsibly, love responsively, act wisely, stay strong. Be well." This requires taking up all of the decayed and excessive aspects of the past and allowing them to fall away from me and gather into piles where they can gently dissolve into fertilizer for new growth—by burning or burial or the gradual effects of being in the open under the sun. The blessing is that my old leaves are changing deeply into new roses.

It is a season to wait on the future with patience and trust.

It is a season to open my hands and let daffodils fall into them.

*Ten*
# The Great Bear

Today the tulip tree over the well is ready to bloom. It is so clear and still that I can hear the river on the other side of the bluffs. Tonight the stars and planets will shimmer in a new moon sky. Only on the stillest days do I remember that I live near a river. It is 'way beyond the meadows I see, and clear out of sight down below, though if the hills were leveled, it would seem a mere walk away.

I like to hold thoughts the way river banks hold water. Land and water co-operate to allow for constant flow, and the one is always being changed by the other. The bank changes because of the movement of water through it, and the water becomes host for what had been part of earth's body, now carried forth by the river in its far-reaching course. I respect and enjoy ideas too much to become ideological. To me, ideology is a closed system, a lake encircled. Indeed, many riches of mineral and plant as well as animal life are held by the living lake. But a lake is alive only if it has some below-surface inlet and outlet and can be fed by fresh water. Without the hidden, opening curves below, the water would stagnate in its closed circle and the lake would die.

On a human level, thought systems stay alive when we preserve our personal boundaries. Intellectual vitality is nurtured by open systems, and by preserving the freedom to change in mutual interplay. When the river is absorbed by the bank it ceases to exist and what remains is drought and parched earth. When the bank is absorbed by the river, earth is engulfed by flood, and land forms drown. River and bank must not identify with one another but work together. The same with ideas and people. Natural changes over the course of a person's intellectual life occur slowly, and though they may sometimes seem dramatic, if they are organic and lasting changes, they will have flowed from a particular mutual interplay between thought and experience, river and bank.

My great-great grandmother was a river woman, an Osage Indian. Family legend is that she taught herself to read and write in three languages and had the strength of all the white men in her new family combined. They called her "Livy"—perhaps short for lively, which she was. I wish I could have sat and rocked with her in front of the fire and learned from listening to her stories. I have only small imagination and some of her blood in my veins to claim the richness of her tradition as my own.

Perhaps it is easier for people blessed with several cultures in their personal histories to refrain from loss of boundaries in issues involving ideas. To know from immediate experience the great enrichment of many thoughts and ways of thinking, of many languages and ways of speaking, is to know that the diminishment of open dialogue between different systems is stupidity and sin. To ignore or disrespect boundaries of thought is to engulf another's ways and so destroy them. It is tragic brutality. Rather when two thought systems are allowed to play and dance together, the purest joys and discoveries are bound to happen.

My artist friend Julia Barkley has opened her dome studio in the sacred Black Hills to be a place of learning between two cultures. White and native artists meet for a week at a time to explore the gifts of the land together—herbs and roots and natural dyes abundant in the old holy places of the American plains. Julia sent me a brochure which has just come in the mail, and I smile to read that one week in July will be an adventure in icons, led by a woman trained in the European traditions of iconography, and a native man whose father was an Episcopal priest and whose grandfather was a medicine man. Rich. Rich. Blessing.

I like to think that it is a blessing of my great-great grandmother that I have a special relationship with bears. My own theology agrees with American Indian ideas and experiences of a holy creation. The North American word which European usurpers rendered into English as "Great Spirit" is more accurately Great Mystery, or Essence. The Essence of All That Is. The Lifesource. The Arabic name, Allah, has the same sense. Though my own name comes from Russia, I take pleasure in believing that its origin is the same, an acknowledgment of our proper relationship to our Creator and a celebration of our creation. When people hear my name, Alla, some are shocked, but I quickly explain, "It is a common Russian name that I get from my common Russian mother." So from both sides I can lay claim to the Bear as my totem: the strong grizzly of North America, to American Indians an icon of the Great Bear, a manifestation in strength of the Great Mystery—and the smaller Siberian black bear of the far steppes, where ancient shamans of Russia followed the patterns of the bear for protection and healing.

The Bear in my life is more than a manifestation of the Great Mystery. It is also the main reason for the redemption of my own childhood. I was one of those troublesome children who was about forty years old at birth and stayed steady at that age well into the twenties. I don't regret that, because my early years were very interesting since I was never kept from adult company, and I learned early on that folks are fascinating because I was permitted to stay up and listen to some of the more remarkable ones: the socialist Norman Thomas, Eleanor Roosevelt, the local Italian consul, United States senators, and so on, because of my father's work in broadcasting then. But also, I was enriched by my mother's friends and relatives from the old country as they spoke in their several languages, and Grandma's earthy shipyard coworkers and boardinghouse roomers. If I was overly solemn as a child, my personality has been growing lighter and more playful since, because at the age of twenty-four, I was introduced to Pooh.

Phil gave me my first *Winnie-the-Pooh* and *The House at Pooh Corner* books a few months into our marriage. We read them out loud together over a three-day period. I was enchanted. Soon I discovered the voices of Pooh and the other animals in the Forest. My oral interpretation professor was surprised when I let down my hair and performed "Chapter Six: In which Pooh Invents a New Game and Eeyore Joins In," for my term performance before Christmas break. At last, I was well on my way to having a happy childhood. My education was rounding out. And just in time!

That Christmas, while Phil and I were wandering through a Sears store in a holiday daze, Pooh reached down from his perch under a sign marked "Boys' Wear" and took me firmly in his paws. The meeting, it turned out, had been pre-arranged between Phil and Pooh. I have been Pooh's human (and quite a paw-full!) ever since. We celebrate Pooh Adoption Day—when Bear adopted us—every year on the winter solstice. That's when the days actually start getting longer, you know, even though we don't really notice it much until that "lengthening light" season of Lent that I spoke of earlier.

Pooh has been a kind of Spirit Helper or guardian angel to me and will remain so for the rest of my life. It's impossible to perpetrate evil around Pooh because his smiling eyes are always there, observing. And to be in foul humor is to silence the Bear, who has to borrow our voices to be heard out loud with his growly counsel or mere kibitzing. And I've discovered that life without growly counsel is too dull for words.

Not only has Pooh seen me through many hard times, helping me when I've lost my bearings, but he's taught me some of the finer points of having fun, too. Hence, the "BEAR UP" message on my car license plate, and the many other Bear-icons and bearaphernalia round the house.

I do not remember having these smaller, calmer angel bears around me as a child, but I own a photograph of baby Alla in her buggy nosing a panda. My mother captioned the picture "Desire." I am respectful of the difference between these relatively domesticated animals and their mortal counterparts, but equally fond of both. So when I was in Washington, D.C., to preside at a funeral liturgy, the family of the person whose life and death we were commemorating expressed their thanks by a visit to the Washington pandas. I had my first lunch with Ling-Ling. I know that she is terrible and fierce in her wild majesty, and the proper way to relate to a giant panda is to respect the creature's need for solitude. I studied panda-nature and came to feel real kinship.

Pandas live among high mountain forests. They are solitary and travel alone except to mate. They enjoy a serene quiet and do not take kindly to interruptions. The perfect animal to inspire writers, poets, and introverts.

When I first came to be with the Mountain I must have thought I was a panda. I even noticed that I was wearing black and white clothing more than my usual brighter colors. But I also discovered something more important than appearances.

I have always known that I am a creature of solitude. I knew that I required eight hours of solitude each day, to pray or write or read or think or watch old movies or just be. But I did not know that I also required six hours of real intimacy! Pooh again. He said it plainly: "It's much more friendly with two."

This is some revelation. Now that I have all the solitude I want, I find I also need intimacy to be creative! I look around at all the bears in my life: Wilbur the Well Bear who guards the well; Aika the soft brown-eyed polar bear who welcomes guests; the silk panda kite which Phil proudly put up in the living room corner; and the many others who encourage me through the day. And they seem politely to restrain some amusement as if to say, "We knew it all along, and she's finally found out for herself," when I make the Big Discovery: I get lonely sometimes; I need other humans, too.

Can you understand when I tell you that finding out this secret makes me more happy than sad? Happy lesson, happy balance: healing comes in solitude, nurturing comes between friends.

## *Eleven*
# Chambered Nautilus

The Beary Godmother flies in a corner of the bedroom. She is a Wise Old Bear with aged-white fur and gold spectacles. She wears a crown with three silver stars. Her wings are made of plumped pink satin, as is the magic wand in her right paw, from which stream forth silver, burgundy, purple, and mauve ribbons in magic Bear Blessing. She began as a beach bear but came home with me from my last visit to begin a new career under the Mountain.

Sometimes, when the sky is cold white and the Mountain colder silver, Angel Mountain becomes a ghost mountain. These are good days for going to the beach. I leave the holy triangle in the morning grey, but if the sky begins to brighten, I am haunted by the thought that the ghosting is gone and I'm missing a spectacular view. By the time I reach the Coast Range the spectre of that possibility has left me. Fickle friend that I can be at such times, I turn my attention to the mountains I'm with at the moment. On a piercingly clear day it is possible to stand near the summit of the Coast Mountains and look across at the entirety of Mt. St. Helens and Mt. Adams from the same spot. Since Mt. St. Helens has been in an eruptive phase, the thrill is often enhanced by the sight of a large plume drifting around her peak, or traces of ash down her sides mapping inner activity as she creates a new dome for herself.

Under the surface of the sea are thousands of creative curves that circle in the ocean in a Ring of Fire as their molten mounds continuously feed the sea creatures and keep a balance of pressure from heat and gas below. There is continuity between land and water here, as the mountains go all the way to the sea and are still being built from below.

I love to take someone to the ocean who has never seen it before, or is seeing this one for the first time. I know the exact place where the road curves through rain forest and the trees open to that first Great View, and though I have seen it hundreds of times, I may still burst into tears at that awesome moment. All the better if I am not blubbering alone.

Made hungry by the last few miles around Saddle Mountain and the first waves of salt air, I aim for the Cannon Beach Bakery or lunch at Lazy Susan's. Then a quick stop at my favorite shop, Crystal Reflections, to scout out a new geode, and after that, a day with the sea. People are respectful of the ocean here, and most do not become so familiar as to speak of "the beach" but talk about "going to the Coast." I feel on more friendly terms, especially since my intimate initiation into the power of the ocean, when I was pulled from a log and nearly swept to Japan over twenty years ago. Never turn your back on The Ocean. If The Mountain is unpredictable, the Ocean is *really* unpredictable. This only adds to the pleasure of walking the beaches. In winter I carry a purple ruffled umbrella for rain, and in summer, a Chinese paper parasol with blue butterflies for the sun, so I can stay out as long as I like and not get too wet or red.

My last walk on the beach was disturbing because I found a seagull's wing, detached by some dog who hadn't finished its meal. I did not like seeing the waste, or being confronted with death, I don't know which, but I felt uneasy until I remembered an idea in a novel I'd read at Christmas. Often we have to tear ourselves away from the evil in our own history, and sometimes we get torn in the process; but it's better to tear ourselves and be reminded of reality by our uneven flight with a torn wing than never to have flown at all.

It is impossible to come here and not think of death as much as of life. Out from Ecola cliffs there is an abandoned lighthouse. It is said to be haunted. After a Portuguese ship, *Lupatia*, wrecked on these shoals over a hundred years ago, no one has been able to stay in the lighthouse. Once a pestilence of storks drove the lighthouse keeper away. Another time it was pelicans. Finally, after years of disuse, the white tower on the rock was purchased and prepared for new use as a mausoleum. If it would no longer hold the living, it might make a good haven for the dead. That seems a most practical application of observing reality with an attentive eye over the years. Someone thought of a way not to waste the structure, salvaged from history to give light of another kind as its gleaming exterior points toward heaven and all maps now warn sailors to steer clear from those cliffs.

On a point immediately south of the lighthouse there is a statue in copper wire to commemorate the Lewis and Clark expedition—Sacajewea pointing out to the ocean, the destination of that westward quest. Light shines through it and makes the figures seem transfigured, especially at sunset when one views the light dissolving into the sea from behind through the figures' coppery bodies. It was begun by a local artist who died suddenly, and his spouse, during the time of her most raw grief, completed the work from pencil sketches, in his loving memory. Love is the link that honors and binds life and death at the core. Love is the power that forms the future from raw or recycled elements of the past. Go down all the way to the sea and find it there also. . . . "And if I go down to the uttermost parts of the sea, and even descend into Sheol, even there your hand will lead me, for you are there also," said the psalmist to a loving God.

Even the light seems honest and loving here, as if it had nowhere else to go and would give itself completely to this one place. The day I was here during high wind in November, the sun was glowing through steel clouds to give the striking effect of a Turner painting, or the rich inner shimmer of a Courbet. I always believed that artists made up those effects, but I saw for the first time with my own eyes a body of water and sky gleam together with a thick golden glow, a tangible, solid color that seemed to emerge from within the substances of the sea and sand, and not at all to come from the silver shadows of opaque but sun-drenched clouds above. Sea, sand, sky, and the same sun penetrating them all and opening them to reflect one another.

Not only is everything connected, but everything overlaps. River and bank, ocean and shore, yin into yang, light into dark, sky into sea, red into gold. Each form has its own body, but at certain points the forms seem to connect so intimately, as if in conjugal union, that the love-making of light between bodies forces us to respect their union at the very point of their boundaries.

There is a sea creature that demonstrates this in its own body. The chambered nautilus lies low on the ocean floor at rest in the dark, or ascends on the powerful propulsion of air through its chambers to the surface of water to bask in light. The creature grows in a spiral form, and as it becomes larger, it builds a new chamber for its new self, always moving in this spiral pattern. But from its smallest self in the center, and from chamber to chamber, the animal carries through the shell walls a siphuncle, like an umbilical cord, for the purpose of convecting air through all the chambers and drawing power from its own origin. Though it cannot go back into former chambers, it remains linked through life with each one of the houses of its own history. It contains all its former selves. And the interconnection through the umbilical siphuncle with its point of origin and all its shapes and sizes is what gives the creature its power to move. It uses air to ascend, descend, and navigate its way through the sea. In a spiral pattern it moves and returns to the same place but from a more distant lateral perspective. The law of constant return and renewal.

And each return is a new birth and a beginning. Each time the nautilus moves into a new pearly chamber, it has to break through the wall of the old one. Passing through the membrane must take great effort, and perhaps pain—the price and the prize of constantly outgrowing one's shell and having to move on. One is never through being born, only complete in each phase of the process.

The chambered nautilus encourages me when I return to places I thought I'd left behind, reminding me that the self I was may have worked through an issue, but the self I am now may have to assimilate it in new terms, as will the new selves I will yet become, and that process is natural and good. Some things in life are linear, but the natural forms are not. Most of life is a gracious curve.

All of the strongest and most enduring structures in creation are curved: the DNA molecule on its endless spiral journey from one generation to a new; the amphitheatres of the Greeks and the aquaducts of the Romans, along with their forum; the living body; the vessels within the body, and its bones; the thinking brain; the molecules of even angular materials; bridges; and the earth itself. What is curved will endure. What is straight will break. Nature knows.

I have a box of note paper decorated on the border by a laser beam which has cut a series of chambered nautiluses into the paper: literal art-by-light. The day before I began my fall drive two thousand miles across country to come here, I sent a message on one of these to a woman in Portland whom I had not met. Her spouse (the priest in the church where I was ordained a deacon years earlier) had died recently after a swim in the Pacific while celebrating their thirtieth wedding anniversary with their daughters at the beach. It was many weeks after I finally met Carol that she told me, as we picnicked in the mountains, that she and her daughters and Larry's sister scattered his ashes from an airplane which had flown them over the Coast Mountains to precisely this sacred spot of ocean at Cannon Beach.

In my first introduction to her, I expressed my care to Carol because I had been told about how wonderful she and Larry were, and grieving then from having never met her spouse, I was determined not to let that happen with her. When I arrived in Oregon the same day as my message, Carol called me. In the course of our conversation I discovered that she had attended my ordination to the priesthood in Philadelphia, when she and her family drove down from New Hampshire where they lived ten years ago. She did not know about my earlier ordination in her present parish. The week prior to receiving my note, her mother was visiting her from Maine, and for some reason she had picked up my book, *Womanpriest*, at the library, and was reading from it to her daughter. When I finally met Carol in person she showed me a letter written by a woman in San Diego who ministered to her family when her spouse died suddenly on their vacation there. This woman also had participated in the Philadelphia ordination service, unbeknownst to Carol, and had hosted me in her home where it was my privilege to celebrate the Eucharist some years ago. All of life's a spiral. . . . Carol wrote me a note this week; she believes that our coming into each other's lives will become greatly significant, perhaps for both of us, but how that will be remains a mystery. . . . Yes. Mystery.

*It was Carol who drove me to the airport to fly back to Minneapolis on the morning that Phil died. She has been an experienced and loving anchor for me in my loss. . . . Everything is connected and somehow in balance or harmony ultimately.*

One day while my house was being painted last summer I went to the beach. When I returned I asked the painter his name so I could write him a check. We both agreed that our names were mutually familiar, and in a few moments' detective work we discovered that when we were children I went to the train station in Portland with my mother to greet his family which was one of the many families she helped to resettle from Germany in the 1950s. I had just hung her pastel of spring roses on the wall he had painted, and I showed him its date—1957, the year he came to the United States! I was thrilled to continue the connection in the next generation. Furthermore, he had just painted the new motel at Cannon Beach where I had been that day. Just a few weeks ago a landscape artist came to prune

my trees, and his name was also familiar. His grandfather homesteaded the road, now named for him,
where my mother's cousins, the first family to come
from Russia and West Germany in her resettlement
efforts, built their own first strawberry farm in Oregon
and started their new lives. All of life's a spiral. . . .

## Chambered Nautilus

Brown as her private parts
pearly nautilus, the seaflower
every woman knows
the deep sea Swimmer
as she knows herself,

each new chamber
earned, she builds
her house around her
an ever perfect fit
to meet expanding life.

No shy daughter
of the deep,

climbing out and out
in well-rounding grace
carrying an umbilical tube
chamber to chamber
for food and air

until, free, she dives
off the edge of her shell
leaving home for good
a beautiful shelter

for creatures
her once own sizes.

In the mirror of water
the Swimmer sees
her sex without walls,
moves her way
into the waiting world.

Angel Mountain is my mother, and this vast and pacific
ocean is my grandmother. When I come to her, I feel
exactly as if I'm going to my grandma's house, where
all shall be well, where everything is contained, and
creation and devastation alike are part of the relentless
mystery of life. Here, I can accept this, knowing that
my momentary raging against death and loss and
change will also be contained by her. Accepted. Held.
Carried forth and back again. Mortality and eternity
meet and marry. And it is always to this precise place
that I come, to my own personal power spot, where for
me life and death are most intensely joined and sharply
focused.

When I am in need of a special power of healing and
strength for myself or others, I come to immerse myself
in the sea, to sing and pray with my body held in her
arms, playing and dancing with her waving music
around me, her wetness all through me—the ocean in
me, and the seer, released by the Sea.

Here I am dancing in the lap of creation, the very
womb of ancient earth, the source of all creatures that live
on this planet, and all who have lived. And at night I
sleep to her growling lullabyes, the ageless roar of the
Mother of the Sea Beasts, the primordial shaman and

shaman-teacher. My Grandmother Ocean. There at the foot of my bed out the window and across the sand is the immense monolith called Haystack Rock, with her two Needles, but which I call Great Grandmother Goddess, Winged-Mountain-in-the-Sea, whose mossy breast is home and nest for a thousand white sea birds. And below, starfish and the pearly nautilus play. Here in play I find the power I need, all ways. Here there is no distinction between prayer and anything else. All is One.

## Mama Sea and Mama Rock

A haystack in the ocean?
A granite mound of seaweed straw?
No—a sea goddess
Mother of the Sea Beasts, rising
for earth and sea children's play.

Oh, the sea frolic of it!
The cavorting on her toes!
Bicycles in ten speeds and sizes
awobble in sand, the wiggles
of Piscean feet let free in the seaground,
erotic dreams of stallions agallop
in spindrift, the leaping legs
of young dogs giddily dancing
after kites, whose foil rainbow tails
twirl through clouds, bright shadows
left on the sky for shooting stars to follow.

The goddess rises, and plays, healed
from old memories of burial at sea,
old losses forgotten in the furrows of her wings.

We climb them and suckle.
She is a breast, a bird, a great mother whale,
old wise woman with mossy kelp hair,
ornamental seagulls are moving white flowers
that sing in her hair—

And the great sea tickle
at her knees, the cosmic applause
of surf for her victories and ours,
the wailing of whales turning
from belly to back to sing
and laugh at this: All mutability,
changeless change.

A woman of twenty dreamily moves through foam,
not lifting her feet, the soft disturbance
of lilac pleats in her skirt, the flowing
blonde down her back in the wind,
the guitar that is silent to wait for a song;
the woman of sixty arm in arm with her friend;
at sunset an old painter makes tracks with her cane;
and eighty-year-old lovers, their arms around each other,
aim straight for the depths, her bright red pantsuit
mocking the red flag on the beach for Danger Today.

I come here to the nest of my origins
on a summer morning,
seabound with a hot sea-hunger,
desperate with thirst for a mountain.
My life thrown open around all life,
full of mountain milk, at last I come
to this water, to drink and to die and give birth.
My eye is fed, and ocean soup, it is good.
Aphrodisiac of Earth!
I am free and fertile,
woman-with-poem again.

O, Mamas, I am here, and I see.
Stilled, I rock and rejoice
in the cradle of life you are.
Leaving the goddess rock to transform
herself into another planet or birth
a star, I move out.

Bowing into the surf
my body that is one
lifts into wave upon wave.
My blood is at home.
I hold the ocean in my arms.

## Twelve
# *Phoenix*

Illumination Rock appears at noon in a thick white sky on the upper right of the western face of the Mountain. It looks like an ear jutting upwards, steely blue ridges forming an entrance into a mysterious sphere. The human ear closely resembles the spiral form of the chambered nautilus, cochlea and inner ear giving understanding and balance to the whole person. The soul draws its power to move itself through time from the ability to hear. Hearing is non-linear. It is an all-at-once perception within the body. The ear cannot scan. It is unable to close itself. Only the mind can shut out meaning. But the ear is at all times receptive. To obey means to hear deeply. To hear deeply in the innermost self is to respond, to move. But the hearing occurs in stillness, when the spiral journey of meaning soulward is clear and unobstructed.

So the prophets of many traditions spoke of "seeing the Word of God" as the inner "I" opened and obeyed the revelation of meaning it received. The Holy One speaks in deepest silence to the inner self.

I am here to see and hear the Word of the Holy One coming down from the illumined ear of the rock. I take shelter in the shadow of a great rock in a weary land, said the psalmist. This Word has new depths of teaching for me. As the Holy One listens to the still throb of my solitary pain, I listen to the throb of divine compassion, and I learn new depths of identity with the birth pangs of all creation.

Faithful to the contract of solitude, I learn more intimately the suffering of empty silence which single people in pain have shared with me from their own labors of living truly alone: I learn the wells of loneliness within inner walls that go down and down into the heart of one's inner mountain, and the sound of a hollow echo when the soul cries out for a companionship that is not there. I learn the fears of the separated and divorced or widowed people cut off from the meaning of mutuality. I learn the depths of self-doubt that come when there is no one to mirror and justify my existence. Is my life of value when I no longer make small sacrifices for another on a daily basis through the most ordinary conditions of living together? Is this new luxury of being able to revel in my own rhythms without constant consideration for the rhythms of another the merest empty echo in the shell of my loneliness? My spouse has shown that he loves me enough to let me go on my creative journey into solitude. It is I who break the contract and violate my own seclusion by calling him long distance before the agreed weekly trysting time, to read from the map of my solitary journey because I cannot bear the ringing echo of my own voice. It resounds in my inner ear and throws me off balance. I want to drive up into town and tell the people at the lunch counter at the drug store about my dreams. But this would be madness. I stick to the black and white clarity of my journal pages as they fill with the content of my soul. I practice fidelity.

Yet with a new humility do I discover deeper levels of my need for human contact. To be lost is to have lost contact. The loss of contact leads to the loss of balance. One wanders dizzily in a lonely desert and grows tired. The soul's fatigue grows from a deep thirst after the depletion of the inner well, a depletion paradoxically caused by lack of use. The way back is through a new use. So the lost often sing and tell stories to the rocks and lizards in order to create new kinds of contact in a limited place. The topography of the soul's desert is flat and bare, until one's eyes and ears learn a new sensitivity to strange forms of life: subtle and harmonious, cactus and dry desert flowers, lizards and coyotes the color of the dry earth, and mountains with neither snow nor green growth. Yet all is alive, even here.

Gradually accustomed to the new sounds and sights, one is rewarded further when that rare day of downpour occurs in even the driest deserts. And suddenly within hours after rain, the desert is in bloom with colors bright enough to burst the eye, and the songs of unseen birds pierce the ear with sweetness. A solitude lived in love can become a blessedly full place, and one's inner desert becomes reforested and flowers with praise.

To discover the freedom of solitude is to overcome isolation. True freedom is always the invitation to respond, and to reach out. A genuine quest through the spiral path leads one to the center, which is the same destination for all of us, though we begin at separate entrances and follow separate destinies toward our ultimate place of meeting. To be faithfully alone is to become all-one with all others. To use the opportunity of solitude to explore inner pathways is to converge at the innermost level with the souls of all beings. It is to embark on an adventure through an amazing inward maze, guided by the light of grace and the still small voice of God's caring presence. Seeing nothing at first, we turn and see the Eye of God upon us, yearning. Hearing nothing at first, we turn and hear the whisper of God, calling. Alone at first, we turn and find a multitude. Yet here we will never be crowded, for we are engaged together in a grand polyphony, each one singing a separate part yet blending marvelously with all the others. And if anyone's solitary song were to cease, the whole sound would be diminished, for the beauty of the whole work depends on the delicate intricacy of each voice contributing to the larger design. We make a desert song and find our way, guided by this swelling music, to the garden of God at the center. We dance along the spiral walls until we find each other.

When I first came here I wondered how I would find or create community. I did not anticipate the warm welcome of my neighbors, or the serendipitous meeting of kindred spirits that happened almost immediately.

Before I even had a mailbox up, I found new friends even as old friendships made that possible.

One day I went to the post office for the mail being held for me. Too lazy to write out my whole name, I handed my card to the woman on the other side of the postal counter. She looked hard at it, then went to fetch my mail. As I opened the first item on the spot, eager for friendly messages, and found a nautilus shell embossed on a lavender card from a woman preparing for ordination in Minnesota, I noticed that the woman behind the counter was watching me intently. When I smiled encouragingly, she spoke up.

"Are you really ordained? Is that the meaning of the title on your card?"

"Yes."

"You must be an answer to my prayer! You see, I have felt a call to ordination for some time, and I've asked God to send me someone I can talk to about it. Will you be my friend?"

How could I resist? God was taking care of both of us. The Holy One had heard our need for each other and led us to find one another. This meeting, and the connection between the woman in whose presence I opened the loving messages from friends far away and the sender of those messages, reminded me of a similar pattern of connection across many miles between women in ministry a few years earlier.

It began with a dream. In my dream I was with a large number of women who were preparing for ordination. I was like a Godmother, brushing their hair to help them prepare for the ceremony, while we casually talked about our experiences of the holy. Everyone went to sleep and the next morning, all gathered to be ordained. I watched as the women walked two by two onto a grassy mound, a round clearing surrounded by tall trees. The women formed a circle, clockwise from left to right, and when all were placed, I heard a direction deep inside to complete the ceremony by ordaining each one with a kiss. I obeyed, moving up in white robes and passing on ministry to each one with a kiss, until the circle was completed and all had been blessed.

When I awakened I felt marvelous, but I had no idea why I had the dream. That afternoon I had a spiritual midwifery/therapy session with one of my clients. She was about to be ordained in the Presbyterian tradition and she had had a disturbing dream in which she was being raped inside a church. We went back into the dream to learn more through active imagination, and Diana said that she noticed a woman peeking from behind a pillar in the church. I invited this woman to show herself. Diana then asked her dream woman her name: "Artemis."

"What do you want?" she continued.

"I want to help you. I am your inner wisdom. I am your source of power. I am the part of you that is always one with the Holy One. If you promise to remember me and listen to me, I will keep you safe. I will let no harm come to you in your ministry, but I will give you power to move effectively. My power is the power of play, of light and dark, and of love. Do you promise to unite with me?"

"I do," said Diana.

"And I promise to protect and empower you," responded her Artemis twin within.

We had witnessed and enacted a profound mystical marriage/ordination rite between the soul and ego, or unconscious and conscious parts of this woman's self. She was ordained in her tradition later that month, truly prepared. The powers of patriarchy were not to prevail or bring harm. Rather she would bring grace and new life into ancient realms and disarm any evil within them.

I remembered my dream, and assumed that it had been a foremembering of this sacred therapeutic encounter, to prepare me for the work of the day from within my own psyche.

About the time of Diana's ordination in Minnesota, I was in the city of Phoenix leading a workshop on the spontaneous creativity of the soul in dreams, fantasies, and bright ideas. The participants were Roman Catholic men and women, many of whom had left their religious orders and institutions, but all of whom felt a strong commitment in ministry, which included helping to create a new vitality in their religious tradition. After leading a guided meditation, I described the creative link between personal dreams and interpersonal relationships by telling the story of my ordination dream and the outcome of working with Diana's dream. The story brought delight and affirmation of the practical application of spiritual gifts, and I enjoyed sharing it, knowing that Diana was happy to have her experience be a source of encouragement to others in claiming their spiritual gifts. The men at this conference were particularly eager to let the women know their support and affirmation of the women's ministries, including what some felt to be the vocation to priestly ministry.

At the conclusion of the conference there was to be a Eucharistic liturgy. The coordinator of the liturgy, a Roman Catholic (male) priest, had asked me to don my priestly vestments and participate. Without giving the invitation too much thought, I vested, but the moment I walked into the chapel to see all the male priests wearing vestments and none of the women except me vested, I saw the reality of the situation. The coordinator wanted me to stand at the altar after the Offertory and consecrate the bread and wine for Communion while the male priests remained in the congregation with their various communities, concelebrating from these stations. What was intended to be a symbol of affirmation had become for me and for the other women present a symbol of division. Instead of the embodied vision of womanly priesthood, I felt like a sacrificial victim behind the altar, unintentionally divided and conquered. There wasn't time to correct the situation by starting to plan it anew, but three of the women who felt as I did agreed to stay with me and be guided by grace as to what to do.

When the time came for me to go to the altar, all four of us went. I then spoke:

"Before we continue, I must call attention to what our actions say. I cannot stand here and lead us in the breaking of bread when my sisters in ministry are separated from me. We claim to be the enlightened ones, yet we act without clarity of thought. It is bad enough when our hierarchies fail to recognize and celebrate the gifts of women in our traditions who are by necessity already offering priestly gifts to the Church, but when we make the same mistake, it is inexcusable. I want to show publicly tonight, lest we belie our own work of the past three days, that we share Christ's priestly ministry together, women and men, of many cultures and traditions, and I share these priestly symbols lest they be rendered false and be put to the evil use of division."

Then I began to take off my vestments.

First, I removed the priestly stole from my shoulders and placed it around the shoulders of the woman on my left, and then kissed her. I removed the cincture from around my waist and girded the woman on my far left with it, and kissed her. I removed my white full-length alb and robed the woman on my right with it and kissed her. I stood in the middle, stripped to my ordinary clothing, and we proceeded together.

Together we pronounced the sacred words, "This is my body. This is my blood." Together our eight hands—brown and white—raised to hold the bread of heaven high to heal God's broken people. Trembling, humbled, together we led our people in giving thanks, and our own tears mingled in the cup of salvation.

Later we were told that a male priest in the congregation had thrown off his vestments, saying, "I won't wear false symbols either." Only later, reflecting quietly in the warm desert night outside, did one of the women put it together with our workshop earlier and say, "Your dream! It was your dream come true! You moved from left to right at the altar and you kissed us! Truly we felt like women ordained tonight." I had forgotten the dream, but now it was clear. My dream was doubly useful, for as well as Diana's ordination, it was a foremembering of this powerful night in a city called Phoenix, when an old reticence burned up within us and we were made a new people, reborn together from the ashes of our fears, of our dead dreams for wholeness. The dreams live again, and even now are coming true. In the dark, we rise, and learn to live in fire.

Millions of years ago in a sea now desert in the middle of this continent there swam chambered nautiluses nine feet wide. The shells of the giants lie underground now, but the desert still lives. It has given way to new creatures: the salamander, which, in legend, is able to live in fire; and the phoenix, a mythic desert creature. The city in the Arizona desert was so named because it was built over the ruins of a more ancient civilization. The place was reborn to humanity as a center for creative culture. How appropriate that it should be in this place that the dreams of many would converge, in common offering of gifts, as an act of obedient praise which the desert itself would hear under the night sky. To be heard and to hear are also signs of being born.

Some years later in Oceanside, California, I was conducting a retreat for a small group of Episcopal women at Mission San Luis Rey. At the periphery of the mission grounds there was a tiny Episcopal chapel. On Sunday morning we went there to make Eucharist. But the chapel was locked, and we were told that a special fire permit was required to hold services inside because the wooden structure was so old that fire danger was high. Disappointed, we walked through the churchyard adjacent to the chapel and found a cleared grave in the sunlight. We read the tombstone. A woman was buried here who had been a deaconess in the diocese of San Diego for many years. Her ministry was long and full, but she did not live to see woman priests or move toward priestly ordination herself. Whether she had wanted to or not we did not know, but we did know that her life and work were part of the pioneering effort that made our ministries possible. We thanked and blessed her as we thanked God and broke bread together, standing reverently on either side of her grave to outline the place where her body rested, her head-stone our altar. The consecrated bread and wine rested over her name and the dates of her birth and death, the words marking the memorial of her ministry. Our communion was with her as well as with each other in Christ. We had all been shut outside because of fire hazards of various kinds at various times and in various ways. But from our combined creative fires, new vitality was coming to the earth.

## Godmothers of a New Creation

We now proclaim the Story
valid and worthwhile.
A dozen years ago
we twelve-less-one,
unbetrayed by taking
history in our hands,
made and shaped a future

in faith and fear
for unknown others.
Now see, our blood
glistens in Easter light.

Now you are coming,
our daughters, descendants,
and you are worthy
of the price.

No longer the female patriarchs
of our fears or past years
(or now in the furnace
of our institutions),

you are women come of age,
seekers of life at the edge,
explorers of inner galaxies,
giving holiness again
to all that lives with
recognition in your eyes
and hands, true channels
of the healing power
of Mother/Father God.

And you are Wisdom Women,
daughters of Hokmah[1],
Ruach[2] in your veins, Spirit
flowing like rivers through
your bodies' words,
prophetic fire still
shining in your faces.

You are old, young,
mothers, daughters,
sisters, lovers.
Not one unwounded
among you.

You bear the mark of the One
Who-gives-birth-with-blood,
Who-rises-wounded-and-gives-life
gently, intently, and truly
unrelenting of the gift
of Cosmos.

Now, our priesthood
having borne us by Grace
again and again through
harrows into heavens,
we stand large in
the Gate of Mystery,
with outstretched arms,
the Christic chalice
overflowing for all
that is new on the Earth.

Moment by moment we accept
our calling as midwife and mother,
healer and lover.
Together.

And so we who came before
now bless you who have come
and are coming, radiant
with God-pregnancy,
we bow before you,
ready and full,
Godmothers of a New Creation.

*At the Foot of the Mountain*

> May you bear well and rise,
> growing ever more
> loving and wise,
> strong from your life-giving
> wounds.

[1] Hokmah—Hebrew word, feminine gender, meaning Divine Wisdom.
[2] Ruach—Hebrew word, feminine gender, meaning Divine Spirit, the source of Creation.

## Thirteen
# Biopoetics

Another bright day after false promises of rain, although the Mountain did not come out to play. A good day for going downtown. First a stop at the hospital overlooking the river to visit my friend Mary, who had surgery this morning. Then over the bridge and up Broadway past the old Paramount Theatre where Grandma and I used to catch the Saturday matinee. It's being renovated from its elegant red rococo to a modern center for the performing arts. My destination today is an art gallery where I have purchased a table created by a local artist, Phyllis Yes— my Yes Table. I call its delicate spiral patterns "lacquer embroidery"—intricate designs of acrylic on wood, in lavender, blue, sea green, and peach. Then home with my new artwork along the freeway.

I am amused at the accidental poetics of a large sign ten miles east of Portland, situated exactly under the

Mountain as one comes to view the large letters on red: FIRESTONE. It certainly is. But I don't think the commercial sign intends to caption the old volcano rising above it. Still, today it draws me to a meditation on stone.

In ancient Greece in the temples of the Mother Goddess, and in Christian churches in Europe dedicated to the Mother of God in the middle ages, there are labyrinthine patterns in stone called the Dromenon. The Greek word is the same from which we derive *drama*—enactment. For the Greeks, the Dromenon was a sacred spiral which one followed on foot, in and around and back and in, until one came to the center. At that point, one was healed and renewed in *re-membering* the Great Mystery and one's place in it. Those who felt weary and broken, dis-membered in spirit, went to the sacred places in order to re-member themselves by this inner journey.

In certain places in England, the Dromenon can still be seen from aerial angles as pathways along hillsides over sacred sites, and in some cases, entire communities still observe the rite of procession together along these labyrinths at special times of the year.

The power of the act was not for the benefit of individuals alone, but for the enhancement of human consciousness, and for the benefit of the whole society through its individuals. Inlaid at the transcepts or crossings marking transition and turning-points, or points of convergence inside the temples and churches, the Dromenon was revered as therapy-in-stone. It was a trance-and-dance to the center-ring, dreamquest from the outside in.

In the same way, people with problems would go to the temple or church to incubate, or sleep, in order to receive wisdom and guidance from God in dreams. It is believed that one of the functions of psychotherapists—or soul-healers—then was to listen to the dreamer tell the dream and to write it down for the person to keep. The dream itself may have had healing power by fore-membering a future solution, assurance of wholeness for the brokenness caused by one's problems.

Both ways held the power to heal: the inner passivity/outer activity of the Dromenon, or the inner activity/outer passivity of the dream. The word *incubation*, for the dream-rite, may derive from a term meaning *to go into the beehive*. Bees show the fertility of the soul, and they have been symbolically associated with the fertility of both the Mother Goddess and the Mother of God, as well as of the Holy Spirit. And they show that both sting and sweetness are elements of Spirit-power.

The Dromenon dance was a turn and return to the matrix of the mother, to the calyx of the flower, to remember the original pulse of life. It was a rebirth of consciousness and a healing of hurts through an unspeakable gift of understanding, an intuitive awakening.

Now my drive is over and my meditation takes me inside my own house to my present work, and as I approach the front door, my thoughts culminate with the buzzing of a thousand honeybees feeding on a huge, white, early-blooming andromeda bush. I smile and hurry in.

In being faithful to my writing, in my own way I am incubating, and also following the Dromenon, depending on the part of my mind taking lead on a given day.

There is a theory behind this practice. It is the theory of vocation. To follow one's vocation is to hear and obey one's innermost call to create one's life in a particular way. Not to obey may lead to stillbirth, or sickness. I am here essentially following my vocation, and consequently, giving a kind of birth, and improving my well-being at the same time. My great longing is that the work will not be to my benefit alone, but because I am part of humanity, the whole may enjoy the health of the part. The birth of books is an art among myriad arts. Nothing special, but every art is special.

Art begins with the acceptance of one's place in the universe: we are all connected to each other at the deepest level, interparticipatory. Each person is an essential part of humankind and of cosmic matter. Each person is a special miracle. This discovery is the basis and impetus for all human creativity. It is the source of healing because it affirms by recognition and cooperation the intrinsic wholeness of all that is.

Life and art are like twin birds in a mirror dance, subtly exchanging lead without interrupting flow, following and playing together in the wide sky of possibility. Let's follow their migratory patterns for a few moments. They are, after all, birds of our own making. They fly around inside us yet evade our grasp. They are organic and electric. Ordinarily our antennae are not tuned to their obvious flight routes, but there are resources to assist us, teachers to show us how to sensitize ourselves to our inner processes and to know them as our own. We have help for remembering the obvious—the first thing we forget, the last thing we perceive. The resources I have in mind are people called shamans, the sensitive seers and healing helpers that live in all cultures and help foster the creative wholemaking energy of their communities.

Shamans are healers above everything, but their means for healing are many: poetry, song, dance, conversation, visual and tactile arts, cooking, story-telling, ritualizing. They preserve the traditions of their people by these means. They are ordinary people whose vocation is to be extraordinarily sensitive. They have insight—they see into things. They are intuitive—they go into things. They see inner relationships and speak from their sense of connection, their vision of essential harmony. They speak the language of nature. They make meaning. They make sense. And when they help others to understand the paths to harmony, they help others to heal themselves.

The modern shamans of North American native tribes believe that what they do, everyone did in the beginning, but the rest of us have forgotten. Their job is to help us to remember our ancient skills: dreaming, singing, laughing, weaving, and so on. They are master technicians of feeling, and they help restore the healing power of feeling to others. Forgetting the old ways has distanced us unnecessarily from the rest of nature and consequently from ourselves, for *we are nature*. It has distanced us from our Creator, and from each other. It has caused our most life-giving relationships to fade and to break. This is not the real way to live. Even our bodies have forgotten that they are blessed and wonderful, and we have lost our health by breaking communion with all living beings, by breaking the Great Harmony. Long ago, before the world was squared off and people were separated from the music within them, there was harmony. Living harmony of plants and animals, rocks and rivers, waters and swimmers. Mountains and stars gave minerals that formed the human body. Human beings breathed forth and returned life to the flowers and trees. Dance and song were one. Time and space were one. Women and men were one. Soul and body were one. Thought and feeling were one. Work and play were one. Being and doing were one. They were not identical, but they were one. And then the Division. All being became separated from itself and, cut off, nothing lived to the full. Division caused the vision to die, and without dreams, people forgot how to create a future from day to day.

When the essential oneness of life and death was dimmed, there was need for new eyes. The seers came. Then the shamans were special in their ability to recognize the old unity. The failure was not in the connections, but in the senses which no longer perceived them. The shamans still had good sense, and they constantly told their senses of truth which kept their people from utterly dying. The shamans were called up out of their own dreams to restore vision to the waking world. They were called to demonstrate that meeting is expressed in a round embrace that celebrates the roundness of the Earth. Through their persistance, the roundness was restored. As they showed, they taught, and as they taught, they healed.

The old ones are still with us, waiting. We still know how to use some of their best tools. These are metaphors, the meaning-maker tools that show something new by putting together two old things so we are forced to see in a new way. When things are put together, everything feels better. Earth grows healthier.

But the putting-together has to happen in a life-giving way, and not just superficially or haphazardly. That is why sensitivity is so important. Only the true combinations will cause that inner "click" of meanfulness and recognition. False combinations will only increase the hurt. Shamans discern true from false by their own experience. Traditionally, they were people who had confronted their own deaths, by being delivered from a life-threatening illness or serious accident. In experiencing symbolic dismemberment and descent into the grave, they had deep need for the grace to remember how to live and be well, and in receiving and using this grace, they ascended to health and returned to life-in-community with new wisdom. The healer's vocation originates in successful self-healing through surrender to divine grace. There is a famous story of a shaman who became very ill as a young person.

The illness progressed, and nothing could be done until the day arrived when the future shaman began to sing. The person began to feel better in the singing, so the singing continued, and so did the recovery. The person grew in the healing arts and accepted the vocation of teaching them to others, and continuing the practice of self-healing by singing. For someone else, it could be poetry or walking or listening to music or hearing stories that has healing power.

In times of stress or illness and as part of the learning experience, shamans might have visions of talking with the dead whose experience of life's mysteries made them wise. The important factor is the shamans' willingness to listen and to learn from all possible sources, and so to enhance communication in life. The willingness is essential, for experience only teaches if we are willing to learn.

It has been said that a shaman is one "who drops down to the bottom of the sea," and the reason for this is to gain contact and to make communication with the creatures who live there, in order to learn more about the healing connections in the universe. The shaman must be a lover of music and of animals, again in order to communicate and to learn from them. At the beginning of a vocation, the future shaman may go through observable changes. The person may meditate more, seek solitude, sleep and dream more, or be absent-minded. These symptoms occur when we are in a transition from one way of seeing and being to another—they are a prelude to a new life. For the shaman, they mark the opening of the place in the soul where a new art can be learned. Then follows an intensive period of preparation. Everything must be strengthened and harmonized: body, mind, memory. The healing must be complete in order to be repeated throughout life, and passed on to others by example.

The life, healing, communication, renewal, and service to which the shamans are called is also the life to which the rest of us are called in a less dramatic way. We too are called and chosen by our Creator to live lives that are in touch with the Life Source. We are elected to creativity, which may flow out of us like the slow lava streams winding along the low mountains of Hawaii, or burst forth like the lively pyroclastic eruptions of the continental volcanoes. The mountains are alive when they are open and flowing, but they are also all different, both in form and content, as are we.

It is up to each of us to claim our unique way of showing our gratitude for abundant life by living joyfully and overflowing ourselves. In every encounter, every significant and insignificant act of our lives, there is the possibility for us to add to the living poem of creation. God is not done with us yet, for we obviously have room for improvement and growth, and all that we do furthers the creation process if we are aware and agree to it.

My friend Mary, who had surgery this morning, reminded me of our unfinished state in a conversation we had on the telephone last evening. She was remarkably alert this afternoon, just hours after anesthesia. I went to give her a kiss, and not for conversation, but she amazed me when she rose from her grogginess to plan with me the details of her recovery:

"I'll just read at first. And you can get ice cream for me, and we'll watch movies. Then later maybe I'll spend some time with you in the mountain house, and I'll paint while you write poetry. In three or four weeks it will be time to think about how to get the finish on my decorated Easter eggs just right. I have to work on the shine. . . ."

And then she fell back into a healing sleep and I left her, dreaming in the sunshine. She has become a shaman. She knows how to heal herself. Her daily job as a clerk in a drug store will have to wait while she tends to her life-making task, and lets me share it with her. Whether hiking to a waterfall with Mary and her family or watching her illuminate an Easter egg, I learn.

Artists of all kinds today often receive their vocations and respond to their gifts as a result of confronting their own deaths, either internally in vision or dream, or externally in illness or accident. I read that a famous young novelist began his work several years ago while recovering from a life-threatening motorcycle accident following the death of a love relationship.

While he was still feverish in a strange hotel room in a foreign city, the entire plot and characters of his first novel came to him at once, and he began to write. He had been quite "normal" before that. Each of us is susceptible to more or less radical change in the wake of life's shock waves. More blessed are the creative changes that heal and give life than the destructive changes that drive us into dead ends.

My neighbor Melody's fine domestic arts of sewing and baking, and my other friends' art of painting leave me in awe. Feeling the confines of my own genre I imagine the art of fiction writing and think of those writers, "How can they *do* that? Create a whole world and people it and sustain it for hundreds of pages? I can't do that! How wonderful of them!" I suppose we usually respect or resent most what we ourselves cannot do—or believe we cannot do. It's more fun and more beneficial to respect, which I do. If one's own art form happens to come easily, it doesn't seem like anything special. I know that mine is special because it doesn't always come easily!

My present vocation leads me to explore the interplay of life and art. Often one is a substitute for the other. It is tragic when an artist asks wistfully, "Am I alive only in my art and not in my life?" Tragic also is the artist who avoids creativity by drowning in the deadening trivialities of daily life devoid of joy. Of course, art and life are also forms of rehearsal for one another. Happy is the relationship between them when one flows into the other or gives energy for the other. My own experience is that life and art mirror each other, actually synchronize. When they are out of sync, one or the other has to wait. To me, the greatest art is the creation of life; not just life on the physical level, though that is the most awesome, but life as dynamic connection, or relationship.

*Biopoetics* means life-making. *Poet* means *maker*, *bio* means *life*. Once I gave a talk on biopoetics and discovered that the program notes showed the word misprinted as biopoetrics. I thought that was a serendipitous improvement, because of the fresh possibility of poet-tricks. Life-making can be pretty tricky. As a vocation, it may require a few tricks to answer.

Making life work is high art, the fundamental art of becoming fully human, fully alive. *Art* derives from the Latin word which means *joint*, like the elbow joint. A bodily joining. Art joins things substantially to give them use and meaning. The art of life-making is the art of meaningful connections and working relationships. It is the art of meeting, and of being-with other beings. It is the art of discovering new being in new relationships. And all creation is available as subject-matter!

Today the shamans among us might be homemakers or grandmothers or engineers or carpenters or students or disabled persons or poets or entertainers or painters or teachers or nurses or physicians or priests, seen and unseen. Occasionally, even a professional caretaker of souls such as a psychotherapist, or spiritual midwife as I prefer to call myself, may show shamanist gifts.

The poet Maya Angelou describes in her autobiography and in a television interview with Bill Moyers how poetry healed her when she was a child. When she was seven-and-a-half years old, she was raped by a man in St. Louis. She called the man's name, and he was apprehended and killed. The child believed that she was responsible for another human being's death, so she silenced herself. For a long time she said not a word, muzzling her soul and muting her mouth in order, she thought, to keep others out of danger. When she was eight years old, a dignified black woman invited her to come inside her beautiful cool home on a hot day. She served the child vanilla cookies and as they drank iced lemonade, she said, "Marguerite," as Maya was then called, "I am going to read to you from this book." It was Dickens' *A Tale of Two Cities*. When the wise older woman began, "It was the best of times, it was the worst of times," the child thought, "I've seen that book at home, but I never knew it sounded like that!" Then the older woman—the shaman—told her for the first of many times, "Poetry is music written for the human voice." She added, "I want you to say a poem out loud." The child began a sacred ritual. She would go to to a safe place—under her grandmother's high bed—and speak poems out loud. The sacred speech of poetry gave her back her voice.

The poet W. H. Auden paid tribute to another poet, William Butler Yeats, by explaining pain as one origin of transforming art: "Mad Ireland hurt you into poetry. . . ." Art is a way of transforming pain, a way of redeeming loss, a way of celebrating reality, and a way of illuminating possibility. I think of the power of Zorba the Greek's exuberant dance in grief, and the power of playing Grieg's Concerto in A Minor on the piano which has healed me of hurt since I was thirteen years old. Blessed gifts, all.

The discipline of my own art is in distinguishing the personal therapy of poetry from the interpersonal poetry of therapy. As a poem-maker, I must also be critic—one who discerns and differentiates—in this case, between words whose music has only the private power to heal me, their speaker/creator, and words whose music arcs publicly beyond the closed personal circle to open and empower others as well. These latter may constitute art, for they truly join poet-as-source with poet-as-resource, those who receive the public published words and sing them anew within their own feeling beings. Similarly, musicians resound music composed by another, and viewers perceive a painting with new eyes in the meeting.

In my book, *The Word's Body: An Incarnational Aesthetic of Interpretation* (The University of Alabama

Press, 1979), I explore the idea that the creativity of the audience is as essential and necessary a contribution to a work of art as the creativity of the original artist. The artist creates but the audience completes the art and makes it work. Those whose primary gift is to appreciate art are as necessary to it as those who create it. The creation circle requires composition and completion: artist and audience.

An actively receptive audience is a full participant in the artwork. Art is a connective link, a completed act of ex-pression/im-pression which we experience in moments of communication or communion. Art is possible only in mutual openness and response between artist and audience: those who join and those who hear. In a sense, *A Tale of Two Cities* was re-created when it opened a powerful possibility for the voice of poetry to a small child in a dark room that summer day long after it was written, and far across the sea from its origin. One artist—Dickens—gave a gift to the world which became the healer and muse for another artist— Angelou. But it took a shaman's skill to arrange the meeting. The poet's gift and vocation came to her when she *heard* the voice of poetry for the first time. Every artist is also an audience!

The connection between art and healing may be *the dynamics of connection itself.* Meaningful connection creates new life and renews wholeness and well-being. If art means joining and healing means whole-making, then art may heal by creating new fullness of being. Wholeness includes and sanctifies (makes holy) brokenness by making it meaningful—useful. So people recovering from illness or injury know they are getting better as they turn to reading, listening to music, noticing beautiful things around them, dressing themselves with color in mind—then to needlepoint or quilting, carpentry or gardening, drawing or writing, baking or singing.

It is also healing merely to be in the presence of art. Those who receive what the artist gives are also artists because they help art to happen—without them there is no joining, no mutuality, but the mere extrusion of something into the void, or the burden of the giver/ artist having to be a solo receiver/audience as well.

I have seen a film showing a Peruvian shaman at work. On Wednesday evenings he would enter an extraordinary state of consciousness in which various artists would paint through the medium of his hands. He was their amenuensis in the communion of saints, taking dictation in form and color. While this happened, the artist or artists would speak through him in their own voices and languages. He was a kind of interdimensional interpreter. He did this ambidextrously so that Leonardo and Raphael could work simultaneously and converse with one another, while the shaman also maintained his own ego state and could intersperse a Spanish phrase into the Italian.

What he said was always of a teaching nature, encouraging people to live good and kindly lives, as if the artists were eager to communicate what they had learned in the realm of eternity with God since their deaths as their natural growth continued. Art critics came from all over the world to verify that the paintings were indeed authentic in the sense that they were true to the natural course and direction in which the artist's work was evolving at the time of death. The significant thing was that people came to sit in the room with the shaman as he worked, and those looking on, without being directly addressed, would experience a change in the atmosphere, a charged and at once serene quality, and those who were ill or distressed left feeling better.

When an intention of goodness and well-being is transmitted into an atmosphere, it fills that atmosphere to the benefit of everyone in it—erasing distinctions, other than functional, between channels and recipients of creativity and healing. When healing is at work, helpers are healed along with those whom they serve. I know that I have not been a clear channel for healing when I feel drained rather than energized after a session with a client. When the creative power of a healing energy fills the environment, I am contained by it along with my client, and both our lives become better. It isn't my own energy that I use—that would be like offering someone my shoes. They wouldn't fit the other person and I'd be left with cold feet. Rather we tap the wellsprings that flow from the heart of God, and feed together on this living water, breathing into our deepest beings the mist of a loving presence whose Spirit fills all available space. All we have to do is create a space, which may mean withdrawing ourselves a little to make room for the Holy Other. Sometimes the most helpful and creative thing is to get out of the way.

One spring several years ago I was with a new friend from another country. We were talking about the therapeutic process, sharing our joy in the self-healing of our clients as we go with them to encourage them on their spiritual journeys. I commented that our job is also that of map reader, for we are most effective when we ourselves have gone the way, even if only the day before. My friend agreed to this, and used the word "therapeutic" but with a new color:

"Yes, it is very *therapoetic*," he said. That would mean *health-making*! His European accent allowed me to see and hear this word in a new way, and so I conceived a deeper connection between creativity and healing through a new concept, serendipitously invented in our conversation. It is believed that, in ancient Greece, the original "therapists"—whom today we regard as healers—were interpreters for the oracles at Delphi. Apparently the inspired speech of the oracles was an unintelligible ecstatic utterance, but these few people had the gift of understanding, and they translated the messages from the gods into normal language so that everyone could benefit: *the poetry of therapy*. It was this final step that was crucial, and that had the power to heal, for it brought people together in the shared understanding of a blessed gift—God is with us and within us, within all life. *Biopoetics* is the way I play in the presence of God.

# Biodance

*everything bears the property of love*

*Sitting on a rock in the Salmon River, Wildwood,
Oregon, watching first leaves fall early in September*

From sunhigh mountain treetops
upstream the rapids carry
old branches to the sea,
their leaves landlocked already.

Why so soon?
Not soon at all—
your time is complete,
and so is mine.

You rest in sunlight
before transforming
into earth and air.

You dissolve your leafy form
and recompose into a thousand bodies.

Nothing ever ends.
Everything is always
    beginning.

Shall I find myself tomorrow
shining in a waterdrop
on a piece of moss
on the bark of a tree
that once was you?

Green into burnt-red,
old leaf, our biodance began
millenia ago, but today
I am glad to see you clearly
for the first time
with just these eyes,
my changing partner!

Your bronze body
turns
to powder
with a crack
beneath my foot.

Part of you has already become me.
You are on your new way.

You will be back.
And so will I.
      So will I.

*Fourteen*
# Marigold

Marigold lived among her mother's people. She was a young Osage woman of fourteen years. Since her mother's death, Marigold of the Osage managed her mother's house by the river. Marigold led two lives. Her first life was ordinary—keeping house, tending the garden, weaving with the elder women. Her second life was secret, lived in sleep. Young Marigold had visions.

For some months now every night in dreams an older but still young lover came to Marigold, proposing marriage. Marigold resisted. "I cannot marry you. You are a sleep spirit. You are not real. You cannot support me. You have no means. I cannot marry you." But the dream lover persisted. Marigold grew sad. Her work faltered. Her play stopped. The old ones noticed. One day one of the women approached. (They had been talking among themselves, the elder ones, the wise women, the crones, and they had guessed her secret.)

At the Foot of the Mountain

"Young one," said the elder, "we see your distress. Come. Tell us what spirit troubles you so you find no rest in sleep."

Marigold denied what the woman suggested. She denied and denied. Finally, the woman gave up and let her be. The dreaming continued.

The dream lover became more and more demanding, and gentle persuasion changed now into terrible threats. "If you do not marry me, I will cause many rains to ruin your people's crops," said the dream lover. "If you do not marry me, I will make you ugly and barren so no mortal will have you," said the dream lover. Marigold had no lawyer! Only her young brother and the older women—but she could not tell them her ridiculous situation.

One day after the beginning of harvest, Marigold fell asleep outside under a cedar tree. In her dream, the cedar tree was burning. It gave off a delicious fragrance as the cedar oil dripped and dissolved from the heat. The perfume from the cedar flames lingered in the air, and though the tree continued to burn, it was not destroyed. Instead, many different kinds of birds were drawn to it because of the sweet aroma. Hundreds of birds began to circle the tree, Marigold still sitting safely under it. The birds began to speak to her.

"Listen," said the first bird, "the one who has been coming to you is no ordinary phantom. You are not being haunted for nothing! We come from the Great Mystery. It is God who has sent us to tell you, since you would not accept the proposal or fear the threats of the other, and we are here to speak, so hear us!"

Marigold nodded, showing her cooperation. The second bird continued, "You have lost your mother, and that is sad for a woman so young. You have grieved much for her. Your father left long before. To you was entrusted the care of your young brother. You have been burdened by death in many ways. The one who comes to you in dreams has been sent to help you. You are meant to marry the holy teacher in your soul. In being faithful to your dream spouse, you will learn all you need to know in life—the secrets of healing, the secrets of child-bearing, of food and flowers, the gifts of creation. You will become mother to your people. For this you were born. If you continue to refuse, your spirit will dry up, your people will go motherless, and you will die. Now listen and obey! You will be protected and taught, and all will be well."

The circle of birds began to unform. The hundreds who had witnessed this meeting flew off in a rainbow of wings, colors made brilliant in the reflection of fire on the sky. The flames drew in and the cedar tree held light and heat without fire. Marigold awakened.

While dozing, her life had changed.

She felt as if all her bones had been removed, washed in the clean river, and one by one put back in her body. She rose and stretched herself. She went home to prepare supper for herself and her brother. She had no dreams that night but slept peacefully for the first time in months. Three nights later, the dream lover returned attired in wedding clothes. Marigold was married.

She learned all that the dream birds had promised and grew in wisdom through the years. She became her

149

people's medicine woman, and all her long life she danced her shaman's dance for healing and sang at births and was faithful to her calling.

Her sleep was never disturbed. Until she died, her hair smelled of cedar smoke.

* * *

Marigold was not the first or the last to resist the inspired demands of her own soul, her vocation. Most of us find one excuse after another to distract ourselves from what we want most deeply. We avoid our heart's desire. We fear the opportunities God gives. We mistrust our dreams. We forge ourselves and drown in the mundane. We deny the obvious direction in which our life is leaning. Better to follow the outward norms and do what is expected and nothing more, we tell ourselves. Better to conform than be transformed.

Even Christ had moments of resistance—intensely so. And not without cause. Christ's vocation was to be a healer, the original meaning of *savior*. To be saved or salved meant to be made well. The savior's vocation has its seeds in surrendering to and surviving death and disintegration, emerging triumphantly in rebirth and reintegration. But the passage can be demanding, even exhausting.

The word for the healer—*sram*, then *shaman*—originally meant "exhausted one," as it came from Sanskrit into Tungusic and Russian. Becoming well is hard work. Being born is even more so, and the shaman is called to be reborn again and again, to show others the way to self-renewal.

To make wholeness of one's life, in relationships, work, and play—this is a vocation common to all of us, and it requires the steady use of all our resources. There is no teacher's manual for healing because each person must learn from the inner teachers the unique means of making wholeness proper to that individual's life. The discovery of a personal journey is what gives us distinctive vocations. Fidelity to the personal process leads us on to a transpersonal pilgrimage in the developing life of the spirit in all creation. The shamans' work could well be exhausting, and their name was a reminder of how to take care of themselves: remember to rest. Living truthfully means remembering one's limitations. The Greek word truth—*alethea*—means to come out of the river of forgetfulness—*lethe*. To live in the truth is to attend.

In the story of Marigold, resistance is a central theme. In the face of a strong calling, resistance is common. Look at the prophets. They were always saying, "You don't mean me, of course, God. I'm too young—or too old. Too stupid—or too smart. You've made a mistake. Please, check your records again and go choose someone else for this job."

Maybe you and I do that, too. We say, "No, no, no. It's too hard. It will take too long. I'm too tired." Even the simplest things, like regular physical exercise, lead to such protests, or more often to passive neglect—forgetfulness. How much more do I carry on if the challenge is to stand up in public for an unpopular cause, or to submit to medical treatment in illness or injury, or to follow through on a creative project! I resist because I know that a certain energy will be required, and I hesitate to make the expenditure. I want to be left alone with my own time; I want to be left alone with my limitations. So when life calls us to transcend our limits a little or a lot, we resist. Too much effort to exercise, or to get well! I want to be left to my laziness. Too much effort to form a new relationship! I want to be left to my loneliness. Too much effort to work for a just cause! I want to be left to my entropy. . . . Yet, that isn't true. I don't want to rot. I don't want to burn down into the perfect balance of death. I don't want to be devoured by my limitations. I don't want to be controlled by my inertia. I choose life!

Then one faces the dangers on the other side. It may be better to burn up than to burn down (though to outsiders the results seem the same) because I will know the difference. Having embraced the challenge, I may burn up too quickly and forget the reality of the need for practical rhythm. The result would be not too different from no action at all, for uncontrolled action also leads to waste.

Among the medicine people of North American Indian tribes there is a common knowledge of the need for practical rhythm. Healing ceremonies are sustained by many rest periods. The shaman who has been dancing and chanting at white heat and the community gathered as a supportive chorus will stop everything at regular intervals, so that everyone can sit down to relax. This means replenishing resources with food and drink, as well as laughter and conversation. When everyone feels filled and good, the prayers begin again. And so it goes through the night until the ritual is ended with the dawn and everyone goes home to sleep. The shaman needs more sleep and more food and drink than anyone, having spent the most energy as presiding choreographer, dancer, and director.

Shamans live in a state of high awareness. It may be a nuisance always to be on call to the holy—available to make healing connections as needed. They need to stay tuned to the internal rhythms of the universe. So one may resist because white-heat-living is not very appealing. But the experienced shamans know that one needs to tune down, too. Even the professional white-hot ones take time out to go to the movies. And they do this to show us by example that rhythm is everything.

Dedication to the sacred can be fatiguing, but the denial of vocation can be worse. The disaster of denial is a loss of the taste for life, a loss of sweet vitality, a loss of the savor of one's daily work. Life can go flat, and the boredom or inertia of being false to oneself, betraying one's gifts and wasting one's time, is the same as having one's soul always under a rock. No rhythm, no breath. A flatness flatter than fatigue—this living death.

Better to take on the challenge and find new interest in it from day to day. Better to keep one's taste for life alive.

And may wise birds visit us in our dreams and our hair smell of cedar smoke until the day we die!

## Fifteen
# *Seven-petaled Lotus*

A mountain bluebird perches on the agate pool rim and regards itself in the water. I imagine how exquisite the scene would be garnished by a seven-petaled pale rose lotus floating in the pool. As I daydream, I touch the silk lotus leaves embroidered on my priestly stole. It was made for me lovingly by Luan, a woman who had walked seven hundred miles through the jungles of Cambodia between South Vietnam and Thailand, where she sat in charge of two thousand Vietnamese refugees on the border at Nong Samet and patiently worked chromatic magic on raw silk. This gift I now keep, and when I wear it to celebrate the sacred mysteries, I remember the remarkable woman who created it for this purpose across the ocean.

My friend Jean, who worships in the Wisdom House community, spent four months as a nurse in the refugee camp through the America Refugee Committee last year. Luan and Jean became friends, and the stole was Jean's gift to me, and a bond for me with a friend whom I have not yet met, but whose story daily inspires me. Red dust from the camp's earthen floor and skin particles from Luan's hands invisibly woven into the lotus pattern make the gift more holy to me. Above the exquisite and patiently crafted shades of rose and emerald on the lotus flowers and leaves are two Chinese characters signifying the Goodness of God and the Mercy of God. The artist's personal life struggle to be free bears testimony to an abiding presence giving strength and guidance. As the lotus rises from the mud and mire of its origin, it breaks through the surface of the water and bares itself to the sunlight, a purified and sturdy flower, thus sacred to the Buddha, the footprint of the Bodhisattva of Divine Compassion.

Luan's dangerous journey through the jungle followed the pattern of the flower, as she herself endured and lifted her head in a hope for freedom. She was true all along to the future contained in the present, the freedom contained even in the hidden and bound soul. I celebrate the Eucharist—the Great Thanksgiving—observing the spiritual seasons, and in each one I am renewed in hope by the lesson of Luan and the lotus flower.

Looking in the water, I reflect on the sacraments of life, the outward and visible signs of inward and spiritual graces, and the interplay between outer and inner forms, my face shining in the rock pool which is in turn reflected in the pools of my own eyes, given the power of sight by virtue of the minerals that come from the stars and give life to my body. I think of the mystery of number, a quality signifying that we live in an ordered universe.

The physicists who believe that everything is made of light, that the light quanta or photons compose the subatomic structures of all matter as the first manifestation of energy, also believe that the number seven is integral in the structure of the universe. The mythology of ancient cultures describes a Seven Storey Mountain as the central axis of the world, culminating in the Pole Star, the navel of the sky, the summit of the universe. I think of the seven days between rest and rest—the quiet climax of Sabbath-time—the seven gifts of the Holy Spirit, the seven colors of the visible light spectrum, the seven chakras or "wheels of energy" uniting physical and spiritual systems in the human body, and seven kinds of silence: of not-knowing, of waiting, of transition, of rest, of listening, of seeing, and of communion. I look at my home under the Mountain, awaiting its brass plate sign, "Wisdom House," and remember that in the Book of Proverbs the House of Wisdom has seven pillars. Among the sacraments of life the Christian tradition singles out seven, which I expand into a metaphor that goes beyond fixed liturgies into the realm of a larger experience of life's mystery.

This is an invitation to explore seven spiritual wonders of the world. Meaning is not a rigidly fixed pattern, but an interplay emerging from the relationships in the momentary joining of these qualities. It is a way of extending the sacraments to see their power in a new way (metaphor).

This is just for play, to see what we can discover. To balance the pattern, I will add the elements of earth, air, fire, and water, plus the human functions of body, soul, and mind, to give a new series of seven, and work them into a new correlation. The seven sacraments of the Christian tradition are baptism, communion, confirmation, marriage, reconciliation, unction, and ordination. The seven chakras in Indian yoga tradition can be regarded as focal points in the human body where physical and spiritual energies unite. Juxtaposing these two symbol systems can be illuminating. In each metaphor, I shall begin with the sacramental symbolism of my own tradition.

At the beginning, baptism—the sacrament of Welcome. The public embrace by one's people. The public gift of one's name. The blessing of water for eternal refreshment. The blessing of earth for rhythmic renewal. The blessing of fire for ease of light and warmth in transformation. The blessing of air for sustaining breath. The utterance by one's people of one's name, the gift of meaning. Gratitude to the Creator for the gift of individual life. Connect with the first chakra at the base of the spine, the energy circle of physical presence in the universe, the gift of body, and security in the body. Connect with the light spectrum and the color red, the color of life-blood. Connect with the element water, the cradle of life in the sea, composed of the same substances as human blood, as the womb which gives forth physical and blessed being. Message: Be happy here, and well-come. You are in caring company. Grow confidently, for you are not alone. You are a member of the family. We're glad you're here!

Flow into communion—the sacrament of Being Together. Celebration of the Great Harmony experienced when two or three or more share the conscious power of the Holy Presence which holds them. Offering of thanks. Outburst of joy. Poignant, pregnant silence. Mutual nurturing. Being the bread of life for each other in the breaking of the Body of God and the passing from hand to hand. Tasting life together, its savor, its flavor—bitter and sweet—precious, delicious, *sensational*. Movement into song. Connect with the second chakra of sensuality and sexuality below the navel, energy circle of shared feeling, loving interflow, and pleasure. Gift of the senses. The high purpose of relationship. Meeting and receiving another. Response in the gift of oneself. The color orange . . . becoming brighter. Connect with earth, its gifts of wheat and grape, by human hands made bread and wine, by the Creator's words, divine Body and Blood—bread of heaven, cup of salvation, good health deep down. We meet, and the bread of life rises in our midst. We eat, and the wine of healing strengthens and warms us. We are filled by a mere taste and swallow, for life is truly rich and its gifts are potent. Message: Enjoy the divine life within and among you. Be nourished together. Practice the pleasures of thanksgiving.

Lead to confirmation—the sacrament of Full Engagement and Empowerment. The individual's adult response to the Creator and the community: I agree to the meaning of my life and my name. I name myself now, expressing my own meaning back to you. I agree to your company. I embrace and return your presence with my own. I stand on my own in your midst and I affirm my desire to be among you, a responsible member of my family. I stand a creature in creation, ready to respond with my own creativity. The high usefulness of my life I give to the larger design of the Holy One. I accept the responsibility of creating, relating, and responding to that which is my own unique destiny. I open myself to the seven gifts of the Holy Spirit: Wisdom, Understanding, Counsel, Strength, Knowledge, Wholeness, and Wonder. Connect with the third chakra at the solar plexus, energy circle of will, where intellect and emotion combine to direct outwardly into power—the ability to act effectively. Its color is yellow, from the solar source. A color expressing thought beyond oneself, as the sun is beyond earth; receiving light and life from this outside source. The confirmation of one's place in the larger system. Openness to the gifts of the Holy Spirit means willing oneself responsible for their use. The element is air, the medium of freedom of thought and freedom of direction, motivated by enlightened feeling. The medium of high exploration. Message: Breathe in the Holy Spirit and be moved to appropriate action. Commit yourself to receive God's gifts and to use them responsibly. Take your place as a competent participant in creation.

Be ready for marriage—the sacrament of Intimate Union. In ancient times marriage meant being bonded through one intimate relationship to the whole community or tribe. Marriage means being deeply connected by being deeply committed. The high union between the parts of the self, marriage of body and mind, celebrated by soul, the child of this union. Passionate embrace between beings born to be better together than alone. Creative embrace, overflowing new life into the community. Connect with the fourth chakra called the love chakra, between the breasts and over the human heart. Its color is green, the life-bearing color of earthly creation, the color of earth loving new being into existance, the color of the power of love to renew. Connect with the function of body, the gift of incarnation, God's word becoming our flesh in an act of longing love that brings us to birth. Our hands become the hands of the Creator, a means for the Creator to touch creation; our love-making the enhancement of the union within God that continuously creates the universe and gives it a body. Message: The blessing of two overflows into three and adds to the universe. Do not fear commitment, but trust in its sustaining power. Dare to love and to bear another as you bare yourself. Intimacy is necessary. The realm of inner exploration.

Also necessary is reconciliation—the vital sacrament of Binding the Broken, realigning the off-track, reconnecting the part with the whole. Again and again, the bonds of deepest intimacy within self and creation will strain and break. One feels cut off from the parts of the self, from others, from creation, from the Creator. One forgets one's place in the whole and suffers under the terrible illusion of being alone. The sacrament of overcoming isolation, healing alienation, reuniting the separated and hurt halves over and over. Each time one is forgiven one's forgetfulness and welcomed home to the whole, the breaks mend more strongly. Scar tissue shows permanently where the joint was broken, and increases the strength of the body in that place. So in relationships. Reconciliation comes through speaking one's need to be forgiven and to forgive, and in mutual utterance, mutual health is restored. Connect with the fifth chakra of communication at the throat, holding the voice, and also the energy circle for creativity and imagination. Its color is blue, the color of calm and hope. Connect with the function of soul, the meeting place where all brokenness is unbearable. The keenly feeling soul moves out of this pain to restore community, within and without, by communicating the state of reality and so changing it. Message: Out of brokenness imagine wholeness; communicate what is and what might be; create community anew. Remember that breakage is inevitable. It teaches in pain. It can make connections stronger in the healing bonds.

Still things break within and deeper healing may be needed, with deeper soothing in holy unction—the sacrament of Profound Touch. The warm balm of no words but the laying on of hands and the blessing of oil: may you grow whole from these wounds, and be comforted as well. Not brokenness between so much as brokenness within must be attended. Connect with the sixth chakra of self-perception in relationship to the whole, called the third eye. Its color is indigo, full-moon-at-midnight-sky. Connect with the function of mind. When the mind opens in memory of past and future, deepest fears may be released, or deepest hates with the hurt they cause, and instead deep hope comes to begin the work of inner health. How the mind sees itself is crucial, the main cooperating physician in the surgical theatre of the soul. Again, not alone, one sees the need for being touched, for being wished well by others. Perception changes and the course of healing flows through opened channels. Others touch with soothing, strengthening hands, so the needy self can receive and use the healing powers of God within. Message: See and remember others who are eager to touch and help you when you need deep healing. These are not the last rites to prepare you for death, but the ever-present rites to remind you that eternal life surrounds you now with all that you need.

Another beginning is ordination—the sacrament of Inner Destiny. The call to what one is meant to be, what gives meaning-to-being. The call from within and without, Creator felt in the marrow and community felt in the many who mirror one's particular service to the whole. The submission to serve. To serve best by being one's truest self, out-goingly. To be lifted up as an icon of creativity and healing, and so a teacher and a helper to other members of the family of creation. Always the questions: how am I called? how can I serve? how best can I use what I have been given? And the trembling recognition of the obligation to respond by saying Yes to the potential. Connect with the crown chakra, the seventh energy circle, sometimes called the thousand-petaled lotus, the center at the top of the spine where human and divine lights interflow inside the dark orb of the skull. When opened, the center of cosmic consciousness and union with God. Its color is violet, and sometimes gold, the reunion of all the preceding colors on the scale of visible light. Its element is fire, the power to transform and purify, the phoenix-nest, the liberator of gold. Message: Become what you are and come alive. Let your passion flow into the compassion of God and become part of the fire that fills and warms the universe without consuming. Breathe yourself into the Holy Spirit and complete your destiny.

One for the *individuality* given at the beginning in baptism.

Two for the *coupling* of communion and the *celebration of differences* in the Great Harmony.

Three for the *movement* into *responsibility* and the formation of destiny that deepens in confirmation.

Four for the *wholeness* of deep connection in the *commitment* of marriage.

Five for the *breaking open* and happy powers of reconciliation.

Six for the *healing and sustaining* of holy unction.

Seven for the mystical fullness of fusing with one's *ordained destiny*.

In these ways, all the sacraments are for everyone.

The specific sacramental moments in my own ministry with others have been rich and interflowing. At Dotty's deathbed, in the sacraments of reconciliation and holy unction she healed her memories and prepared for her last journey on earth. I asked what she felt remained unfinished in her life that still held her here, or caused her to leave with regret. She said her daughter was still in the harrowing environment of graduate school in geology, a science not known for its hospitality to women scholars. She regretted not being able to give Holly emotional support through her last two years of study.

Out of that came a Eucharist around Dotty's bed with her spouse and two daughters, during which I adopted Holly as a Goddaughter, promising to offer spiritual support in addition to that of her parents. Holly's older sister Heather and their mother Dotty had been at my ordination to the priesthood some years earlier. Our relationship led us to this holy moment together. Later I celebrated Dotty's funeral liturgy in the family parish in Maryland. Now Holly is in her final year of study in California and has just called to ask me to officiate at her wedding, for she found a loving geophysicist with whom to share life on the earth. These bonds already contain most of the sacraments.

My priestly relationship with Glo is similar. It was my privilege also to help her to die well. Yellow roses at the memorial service expressed her bright and lively personality. Several months later, there were yellow roses at her daughter Mary's wedding, which I solemnized and blessed. Two years later I was invited to bless a tree that Glo's new son-in-law Dick planted in their front yard in Glo's memory. I gave the young mountain ash a pat as I left, and Mary's last words to me were, "Maybe we'll see you soon for a baptism!"

The sacraments are lenses that focus on life, mirrors that intensify our reflection of life. The sacraments, too, make natural and supernatural spirals and cannot be too separated from each other. All the links are inside. I see that, every time I stand at the altar to celebrate the sacrament of communion, and feel Holly's picture of the live volcano over my shoulder . . . and the lotus petals on my stole brush against the edge of the table of our communion with the Whole.

# Where Life Begins

*. . . not in tidal pools but*
*in the thermal vents between*
*earth's shifting plates in*
*the Ring of Fire*

The urges of Earth
are there:
in the hot, hidden
down-under places

between worlds
where surface meets
surface and melts
in the Opening.

This, then, is
the cosmic kiss
where all that
is hard touches
its own Other,
transforms
enticingly,
consummates
and makes
the Never-before.

Where no sun gives light,
no micron escapes
the Divine Fire
from Within, surging
and frothing to come forth

and secret clay
crystals merge

and marry
in such wet heat
of Meeting.

This is where
life Begins
then:
neither here nor there,
but all ways Between.

*Sixteen*
# Invisible Wings

Chinese zither music on public radio's "Midday Modulations." Missing my grand piano in Minneapolis, I dance over the spun-honey carpet where it will reign someday. A small brown musical growler named Pachelbear smiles up at me. Now down into the yoga movement of Invisible Wings, the slow sensual circles flowing with a song called "Lunar Pond," and close with Reintegration.

The equinox approaches, and with the vernal festival, the virginal Feast of the Annunciation. An angel opened its wings to a young woman and proclaimed her fertile, defying the known laws of nature. How limited our knowledge of nature's laws. Do not all of us conceive spontaneously when our souls spring forth with ideas? The artist practices parthenogenesis. The artist enters the vulnerable state, open to the shudder of invisible wings that might announce the new life of a creative work. In no one's possession—virginal—the artist awaits the descending and ascending Presence, and in the spring season, conceives by the Holy Spirit a child of the soul.

Each individual is called to discover a particular art, a special ability that gives power and pleasure. It may be baking or fixing or speaking or listening—special ways of art as joining. Those who identify with their art and make their play work for them and others are proclaimed artists by the public. The people who lived in this house before me were great bakers. I keep my poems in the kitchen cupboard where my predecessor kept her electric mixer. It is merely a matter of vocation. I must remember the different use of my manuscript pages, which would go flying back into chaos should I inadvertently release the hidden spring that raises the cupboard shelf from knee-to-hand level!

How we treat our angels is also a matter of individual whim. We may wrestle with them, as did Jacob, and say "I will not let you go until you bless me," or we may open ourselves like Mary and say "May the life you proclaim within me be true." So we respond variously to our friends and family and teachers who tell us to do our work and fulfill our vocation. And they—these angels in our lives—may tell us variously as well: by urging, goading, challenging, encouraging, scoffing, cajoling, mocking, railing, shaming, pleading, or praising. We wrestle on until we open and are blessed in the art itself.

The artist confronts internal and external problems, and most of these are problems of attitude. A large external problem is the general attitude of society that is reflected in the poet W. H. Auden's comment that art has no social value. He expressed the idea that poetry is a very personal craft and not a political or polemical tool. I disagree with the idea of the separation between private and public, political and personal work, because of the dynamic interrelated nature of all that is.

One morning in May a few years ago I was presenting a paper on a non-linear view of the future, a spiral image of theological process, to a group of professional pastors and theologians at St. John's University in Collegeville, Minnesota. Near the end of my paper I publicly refuted Auden's remark, saying "Auden, you were wrong when you said that art changes nothing. Art changes attitude and attitude changes action and action changes culture, and when culture changes, everything is changed!"

I looked up from my paper to see on the wall of the president's room right in front of me a photograph of Auden himself, laughing and in that very room years earlier, a coffee cup in front of him! I laughed back and raised my own coffee cup in toast to a brother poet, transcending the distance of time in the same space! We were children of our culture, poets interplaying with our times. I pointed out that culture begins with cult, the determination of the nature of a given group on the basis of what it worships—gives worth to. Artists shape culture by showing what the culture values, and what it values most, it worships. Artists speak to conscience when they show the disconnections and false values of the time artistically, or when they celebrate the connections and true values that bind society for the common good.

Then there is the puzzling paradox of the writer's craft, perhaps shared by other fine artists, as opposed to performing artists who usually prepare as well as perform in consort or concert. The writer's process is isolating, but the product is exhibitionist. The innermost and private self is often surgically exposed through the art, but the artist remains detached from this reality. The process is introverted, but the product is extroverted, flower petals shooting outward from the still-confined calyx, striving for the stars. The reality of being known intimately in a public way by thousands or millions of strangers whom one will never know in return—that remains incomprehensible, even illusory, to the artist, struggling alone in her kitchen corner to wrench the truest words (or colors) from her soul, to help increase the authenticity, maturity, and purity of her own creative life and work, and hence of the totality of creation.

Other public problems emerge from the paradox that the artist may be more intimately known by strangers through the artwork than by that person's family or friends and colleagues. Art is the work of soul, and when it shifts from play to purpose, it becomes public property, so that one's most personal self becomes the product delivered to the world. The artwork is then as vulnerable as a newborn child, and the artist as parent of that child needs to learn detachment from it over and over, to avoid the dangers of ego identification and inflation from praise for the work, or deflation from rejection of the work.

The artist needs to be careful to preserve the boundary between the private process of art and the public domain to which the art product is given. I know from personal experience, and from that of my friends and colleagues, the particular vulnerability felt by artists who are pastors, teachers, poets, painters, or performers. If the boundary is disrespected or dissolved, the artist can be destroyed by praise or criticism alike.

The public will do its best to blur the distinction between the artist and the artwork, especially if the artist's main instrument is part of the body, such as the voice, or the whole body in dance or drama. Yet the artist's main instrument, regardless of the type of art, is soul—the feeling function of the individual. Work that comes from ego is usually apparent in its flatness and shortness of life. Soul-work sustains and becomes part of the body of the culture, like a child accepted by a school and later graduated by that school into the larger world. Ego-work remains at home or soon returns home, and eventually the parent tires of its shallow child and it is forgotten. But soul-work matters. It is matter en-souled. And it is vulnerable, as any living thing.

There is a dangerously false human tendency to imagine our Creator as a kind of puppeteer, manipulating creation. There is another dangerously false human tendency to imagine that artists, including helpers and healers, are small idols of the Creator, so we place these lesser gods on pedestals, but we make them our public puppets. This happens when fans idolize and inflate the image of an artist, or when individual fans give in to the illusion that they possess the idol: Artist-as-object. Then the cult around the artist becomes a destructive force motivated by its need for a false god whom it can control. When control fails, the puppet-idol falls from a glass pedestal that may be kicked and toppled quite violently. The result of this set-up is a down-fall. The illusion must be destroyed, for the artist is in danger of being a sacrificial victim, if not to the illusion/idolatry itself, then to its necessary and ultimate dissolution. Every artist needs to guard against this, because it can happen so insidiously, and whether it happens because of many public worshipers or one idolizing friend, the result to the artist and the work is disastrous.

There is a human tendency also to project disowned talent or disowned evil alike onto artists. The artist is again depersonalized into a mirror by the public, and "we do not see things as they are, we see things as we are," as the Talmud says. The artist can so easily magnetize these dangerous and one-dimensional projections, and when the truth of the artist's human nature and three-or-four-dimensional individuality are revealed, the disappointed public can become vengeful. Then, if work and artist are identified, the public will reject the artist as a person along with the art product.

Whether the fragile glass pedestal is toppled or the fragile glass image is shattered, the artist is in neither of these. Only if the artist forgets boundaries and believes the projection or accepts the possession, can the eventual destruction of those things devastate the artist's person. I am careful to remember my own personal reality and keep parental distance from the work I create, and because I do not experience myself on a pedestal above others, I don't fall when it falls. Because I do not believe in the image projected onto me, I am not shattered when it is shattered. Because I do not surrender myself into public possession, I am not desolate when the public abandons my work. But—I remain highly vulnerable as a person to the effects of rejection.

The people called to public art, to be priests or poets in public practice, are ironically most vulnerable to public anger and rejection and most unable to cope with it. The sensitivity required from a good artist is the same trait that will cause the artist to feel keenly every response to the gifts of soul which the artist presents to the world. Because I am careful not to climb up on a treacherous glass pedestal or thin myself onto a flat glass image, I am not destroyed by the falsity of these. But if others place me there, I am bound to fail their expectations and my human nature will betray the idolatry, which may anger those who created it. Then I may get hit hard and cut deeply by flying glass when the crash occurs. I need time, then, to recover my sense of who I am, a vulnerable person and nothing more, among the rest of humankind. I do not want false power that makes people fear to disagree with me. I want my ideas or my works to be rejected if they fail or lose their use, and not myself. And the responsibility to remember the difference remains mine, even when others forget.

Art is erotic. It is a sensual way of reaching out to touch others deeply, to communicate intimately, to stand exposed before an unseen, unknown other in a tremendous act of trust that one will be accepted and loved. Love me in my work, asks the artist. I offer you love through my work, declares the artist. I am not the work, but my life is in the work. My time and my longing are in the work. My dreams and deepest vulnerability are in the work. So there is great ambivalence: dare I complete this work and allow the world to see and touch it? Shall I guard the work instead by keeping it to myself, or aborting it? Shall I be the mother cat who protects her threatened kittens by eating them? These are the internal problems the artist confronts. And there are more.

Mary Artemis is a painter. One night she dreamed she had a lover who kissed her so deeply and intensely that she felt the kiss through her whole body down into her soles. She appeared to me to have been impregnated by the soul-kiss of her dream lover. Yet she put off going to her studio. She felt guilty in taking the time away from her family to be in this other relationship. She feared the erotics of their art! One craves to connect through one's art. She told me she longed to bring her husband to her studio and have him sweep her off her feet and spin her through the air in a passionate embrace in the domain of her art. But that was to confuse her dream lover with her mate. They were two different beings who were not in competition for her, because each related to a part of her unknown to the other and essentially unneeded by the other. Her husband, of course, could not react in the way she wanted in seeing the unknown environment of her art for the first time. He reacted with polite interest and a certain reserve, for he had entered a strange world and did not know how to speak and move in it. Nor could the dream lover praise her cooking in her other world!

She needed to know what each world required and what each lover was capable of giving and receiving from her, and not to worry about them impinging on each other, because they could not, except in the confusion of her mind. She needed to honor the inner boundaries of her separate realities and allow them to exist and thrive side by side. She could have been crushed by her husband's failure to respond in the actualized realm of her dream—her art studio. Instead, and over time, she discovered the right to discriminate and the need to discern the appropriate people to invite into her creative place, making art with those who share a similar craft and can *see* her work with inner recognition from their own creative worlds. Nurtured by those who understood the intimacy of her creative world from their own experience, she then felt strong enough to show the fruit of that intimacy to others, to allow friends and strangers glimpses of the children born from union with her dream lover.

And she learned that this union was not a threat to her actual mortal marriage, but a gift to it, making her humanity more lively and ultimately more accessible to the people in her life. Mary Artemis found that she could function in other art forms that would include her husband. They began skating together, art-fully moving along in the dance of their marriage—which would have remained on thin ice if she had continued to feel the threatening confusion within her!

I feel blessed in collaboration with my friends who are visual artists. Twice I have performed poetry to accompany Julia's paintings in public openings—for

"Energy of Miracles" and "Circle of Fire," both verbal and visual shows. And her drawings have danced among my poems in our book, *In the Name of the Bee & the Bear & the Butterfly*. It is easier for me to work with an artist in another medium, because energies that are too similar can bump into each other, and it takes more concentration to keep out of the way of another poet. Instinctively I refrain from such a collaboration most of the time, because I have discovered its difficulties in an area with which I do not identify—music. The fact that I can play the piano at all is a happy result of being a feeling person, and not the consequence of manual skill. I think of myself as a mechanical moron with little physical dexterity. But I love to dance, so long as I don't have to coordinate with a partner, and I love to play the piano so long as I don't have to count.

My love for my old friend, Alice, the physician whom I mentioned in "Humus," led me to agree to try to play Beethoven's First Symphony in duet with her. At first it was sheer torture. For twenty years I had been playing on the power of feeling and intuition, and now I *had* to play by logic. The fullest art is a process combining all powers—thinking, feeling, sensing, intuiting. But playing the piano has never been a public art for me, only a private source of pleasure and self-healing nurture and renewal. So I was not concerned with using all my powers to make a full art form in my music. I could let myself be lazy and stick to feeling and intuiting.

Having to think numerically and sense my place in relationship to my partner's employed a part of my mind and motor skill that were new here. I felt as if I were literally spraining my brain. As the notes pierced into my mind from the score, I sweated the music out of me: "*One*-un *an*-und *two*-oo-*an*-und . . ." trying to figure out the duration of a dotted thirty-second note in six-eight time! I had to learn music all over again as a system of *logical* relationship rather than *felt* relationship. My relationship with Alice was worth the headaches this caused me. But I was paying a price, for my own way was slipping. I wasn't able to combine the two ways, and when I went back to my solitary piano to play in private, I became all thumbs. This *did* cause me some grief. Since the piano is not my main vocation as a public art form, I had not the ability to use both parts of my brain at the same time, and I was losing the part that I most needed for the personal gift that piano playing had been to me.

Ironically, I got back the gift when Alice died, because I grieved for her at the piano. I had wanted to play and sing the song "Memory" to her a few days before her death, but she felt too low and would not let me come. So the morning after her death, while her nieces and nephews were lovingly ordering her environment, I went to make music in her house for the last time. Overcoming my usual shyness at playing or singing in front of others, I sat down at her old Steinway on the sunporch and played and sang my heart out to her spirit, without once counting. My fingers flowed and flew as through water and air, all feeling again. When her niece asked me if I wanted to keep her duet books, I declined. It was our relationship that enabled me to forfeit my own ways and needs for a time. I may not do it again, but I'm glad I could do it at all, just for love.

The challenge is to be faithful to our dream lovers, and also to our friends and mortal lovers. We are all akin, part of the family, and any family member's gifts bring joy to the whole when it is functioning healthily. Sometimes we don't see this clearly enough, and we allow our gifts to recede. We grow fearful when life or art seem incongruous or inconsistent. It is because our vision is limited and we cannot see the whole picture at once, and how all the parts fit together ultimately. Life *is* inconsistent. Nature mixes her metaphors *ad lib*. Things can't be expected to repeat themselves in the same way. Nevertheless, faithfulness—to ourselves, our gifts and vocations, our friends and relations—is possible. Every time I make love is different from all the other times. Every time I make a poem is different from all the other times. Every time I visit a friend is different from all the other times. Every time I play the piano is different from all the other times. This very inconsistency is what keeps things lively. Variation gives rhythm, and rhythm gives energy and interest, and these give life to any relationship.

The most compelling parts of the Great Harmony are the moments of pure polyphony, when the many voices vary into irregular patterns that blend more marvelously than possible in a more predictable conformity. Nature loves variety. Everything fits together in complex and intricate ways. We are complicated, a symptom of high evolution. And it is acceptable. It is remarkable. A richly textured tapestry woven from infinite varieties of colors and threads, by a master Creator, the eternally experienced Artist we call God. We all fit! It's all right if we happen to be part of the mess that's lying tangled on the floor at the moment, and we are too small and too immersed to see the pattern already formed above us and our own place in it when it's done. We aren't finished yet! We are God's work-in-progress.

So all artists and all artings need faith in the future. That comes with the natural gift of intuition. Sensation is a function of the present, that perceives the details of *what is now*. Intuition is a function of the future, that perceives the whole pattern and *what can become*. Just because I can't see the larger order and consistency of the completed miracle doesn't mean that I can't trust the process and enjoy the small miracles from moment to messy moment as we become the form we're meant to be!

It is a matter of letting light break through us—again. We ourselves are prisms, multifaceted and deep. Light shines and flows through us like water, like fine crystal. Yet each of us is an infinitesimal prism cell fitted into the Large Prism we cannot see because we are too small a part of it. We may detach and step back to observe ourselves and the whole, but then we will see at best one angle of a many-angled Reality, and as light breaks through into our single perspective we need to remember, "This is a *part*, this is only a *part* of the whole miracle!" We are in trouble only when we mistake the part for the whole. Too limited! Consider the variables with as many functions as we can—thought, feeling, sensation, intuition, memory—and we'll be all right.

I commit myself again to overcome my self-created limitations: needless guilt that comes from confusion (or from frightened and confused others who feel needlessly threatened); and my own fear of separation and loneliness in my art; my fear of rejection; my fear of the unknown; my fear of being abandoned by the art itself. All of these things can affect my starter button. A defective starter button is the greatest deterrence to any artist, and some of the loose wires above are more often responsible than not. A quick check under the hood can tell which wires are crossed and keeping things stalled. Once we identify the inner problem we can soon get under way. The outer problems we simply need to keep steering clear of.

Art is relationship. Pooh described it best:

> "But it isn't easy," said Pooh to himself, as he looked at what had once been Owl's house. "Because Poetry and Hums aren't things which you get, they're things which get *you*. And all you can do is to go where they can find you."
>
> He waited hopefully. . . .
>
> "Well," said Pooh after a long wait, "I shall begin '*Here lies a tree*' because it does, and then I'll see what happens."
>
> . . . "So there it is," said Pooh, when he had sung this to himself three times. "It's come different from what I thought it would, but it's come. Now I must go and sing it to Piglet."

One day Mary Artemis went to her studio so her
painting could find her. Nothing happened. Stuck
starter button. She had a cup of coffee with a colleague
instead. That was part of arting, too! Later, while
visiting, she looked at a painting of her own out of the
corner of her eye and thought, "I like that!" She never
had liked it before when she looked at it straight on.
Some things have to be glimpsed from the side to show
themselves, because they are too shy to be seen directly.
Still later she went back and her new painting finally
found her. It came differently from what she thought,
but it came.

When I came here I had no idea what would happen.
I hoped that I would be able to write a book about the
healing power of the creative process. I jokingly said to
a neighbor, "Maybe it won't ever come, and I'll just sit
down and write about the Mountain instead." What a
surprise when both things happened! But I had to wait
and wait, even once I got in the right place. I had to
fuss around with the garden and the leaky roof and
cooking and shopping and calling my friends. Then
when I'd given up and tried to accept my failure
gracefully, it attacked me one night when I fell victim
to Beauty—the full moon coming up over the Mountain
and words of hope and longing poured out of me. Yet

the book didn't come all at once, the way I was feeling it. The inner life was fully formed but I had to let it out of me line by line, the obedient and attentive amenuensis of my own soul. Some things truly are linear. Still, I remembered Pooh's advice. I began by putting myself where I thought the book had a chance of finding me.

The foot of the Mountain is my studio, and there I went. I waited and nothing happened, so I waited some more, and meanwhile did lots of other connecting, which turned out to be an essential part of this book. The twelve hours I spend stewing and dreaming for every hour I spend writing are just as much a vital part of the process as the typing is.

The next thing after waiting was just to begin. The Mountain grabbed me by the eyes one night, and I began: "She is my medicine woman," because she is. Then every day after that I had to keep on hoping something more would happen, and after some daily fussing and waiting, it does. And it never ceases to amaze me. Does every artist look at her work and think, "Where did it come from?"

One night recently I dreamed that I was questioning a woman during her ordination ceremony. She wore silver, the color of protection, and blue, for communication and creative imagination. She was the part of me that was ordained to write. I asked four questions which she answered two ways:

Question: "What do you wish?"

Answer: "I wish to be healed."
"I wish all my pain to be transformed into fulfillment."

Question: "To whom will you give yourself?"


Answer:"To God."
   "To my own Beloved, and to my friends."


Question: "How will you protect yourself?"


Answer: "By remembering boundaries, and lessons of
      the past."
      "I will be more aware of my own needs."


Question: "How will you renew yourself?"


Answer: "By rest and solitary prayer, and with friends."
      "I will make another home for my soul."


My dream priest was directing me on how I should wait. Some of the answers puzzle me, yet I contemplate them and learn. I have learned that there is a time and place for creation, and they are not always revealed to me, but can take me by surprise. Yet my preparation is not wasted. If I set a time and go to a place and nothing happens—it's usually because something else happens that I don't expect, and that something, whatever it is, usually finds its own place in the work later on when it finally decides to show itself and put *me* to work. Maybe I have to wait for years. And maybe I have to let go a lot of what I had planned. That's all right. Meanwhile, I place myself as often as I can in the presence of art—the workings of creation in people and things and ideas. I go to where something might happen, something stimulate something else, something get tickled, stirred up, a place where a Muse might find me, a place where one might get a-mused, and I wait, and do other things, and wait, and finally begin. . . .

Now hours have passed, and the music over the radio is made by an Irish Harp. It ends, and the announcer's voice says, "That was a Gaelic song called . . . 'Invisible Wings'!"

*Seventeen*
# A Happy Childhood

I am typing by the heater in front of the Mountain-facing window in the southeast corner of the kitchen, curled around my words and work like a mother bear in hibernation. Today I dream and breathe them out of me. (Sometimes in the night I awaken in a cold room, hot and sweating from the labors of my dreams. . . .) All around me are sustaining images: The life outside, moving in the corner of my eye. On the east wall in my corner, an icon of the Great Bear carved in pine by a local artist—the Bear is smiling, and large. On the south wall over my head, an image of the Risen Christ, arms outstretched in priestly blessing and angelic embrace, formed by my father from clay on wood thirty years ago. Next to it, a wreath my friend Julia made of grape vines and silk, wheat, and ceramic figures imaging the trinity of Sanctifier, Creator, and Healer—as buzzing-awake Bee, Mother Bear-in-birth, and dying-reborn Butterfly. Then a ship's clock shows me the flow through time, and on the other side of it, on the west wall, is a painting of Mission San Antonio by my mother. I found it in her attic after her death, unframed. She must have considered it to be unfinished . . . or saved it for a surprise for me, like the Christmas gift I received from my father from London after his death—a small porcelain box with birds on the lid I used to save a few fragments of his bone.

My parents were amateur artists—they engaged in art for the love and pleasure of it: *art amour*. It was in their arts that they played and taught me to play. Their professional lives were quite serious. Professional work is art declared a medium for public use, and for the exchange of life-sustaining energy: the personal gift of one's work to the world, and the public gift of money to the working person in return.

Depending on art for one's living is not the same as depending on art for one's life, though a person might indeed have both needs.

Earning one's living through work need not take the life out of it, and what will keep that from happening is the preservation of a fundamentally amateur attitude: *love* of the work, and pleasure in the work. Love and pleasure need not be confined to play alone, but make work even more rewarding than the public purpose for which it is dedicated. When one does not depend on one's art for a living, one is free to enjoy it as a gift. For those who have to live by art—keep the gift anyway!

The enemy of art and life is the illusion of perfection—perfectionism. We need to remind ourselves that we are not God, and only God has the right to be perfect. The joy is that even God, who has the right, seems to choose not to use it—probably because even God finds perfection boring! When something is supposedly perfect, there is no room left for growth. It has come to a dead end. The Creator likes to leave room for improvement, and the interest of what may come up in the process. The unfinished state is what keeps things going. Any created work remains working because every time it is experienced it is new. Art remains art whenever anyone becomes engaged with it, because every relationship is new, and within a relationship new things happen to keep it alive. So in a sense there is no product, only a continuing process focused on the material gift, the body given forth, just as the birth of a child is not the finish of a life, but the beginning: now anything can happen. The process is the product. We destroy the joy and excitement of this ongoing process of continuing creation when we strive for perfection, which is both unattainable and inappropriate. Setting an unrealistic goal for ourselves, we condemn ourselves to failure and frustration, reinforcing feelings of inadequacy and defeat.

To be perfect means be *done through* (*per facere*). To be done through means that nothing more can happen. To be done and finished is to be dead and gone. To be done through is to be done in by an attitude that such a thing is possible! Think of the artist who says, "Well, *that's* done!" and walks away—leaving the painting wet on the easel—to abandon and forget the gift forever! Or the mother who says, "Well *that* birth is over!" and leaves the newborn child to itself. The child dies. The work dies. The gift is betrayed. What comes after the birth of a child of the body, soul, or mind, is the realization that there is a new life and presence in the world to be nurtured and enjoyed. There remains a responsibility to nurture and enjoy that which is part of creation. Our creation doesn't end until the day we die, and even then it only changes so drastically that we simply have no way of understanding it. The same with all work—it has to keep working. Art keeps "arting." It is an active gift in our midst, and it and we are actively fulfilled again and again in every meeting.

The North American Indian artists sacramentalized this truth by leaving a deliberate mistake in a work of art—in bead work, the missing or flawed Spirit Bead shows that the Creator alone has the right to perfection. But the fact that the Creator makes us shows that perfection is not a principle put to use in the universe!

Now it is true that on the subatomic or microscopic scales there is such a thing as the principle of completion at work. Completion means to be filled with the energy of the Creator. A work is complete when it is filled with the artist's creative energy. It is pure in this way, also: nothing is imposed, taken away, or withheld, but all that belongs to the gift is given to it. Its own pure nature is not altered with substitutions or subtractions or contaminated with additions that do not belong to it. I prefer to live by completion in reality than by perfection in fantasy. Completion is all the parts playing their best role in the whole. And from moment to moment, the roles may change, for the good of the living whole.

That is why it is important to remember that just because you're good at something doesn't mean that you have to do it. Many people are multitalented or multicompetent, but they are not obligated to give equal commitment to all of their gifts. They are free to discern and to choose from among them those which give them nurture and joy in return. Our vocations do not call us to cramp ourselves in unsatisfying tasks just because we're good at them. They have to be good for us as well. Only if both parts are true will the good of the whole be served. My mother was an excellent flower painter, but she struggled unsuccessfully with proportion when it came to figures. And she cooked and baked superbly, and designed and sewed meticulously, but these skills and gifts gave her less joy than aggravation. Always challenging herself to do what was difficult, she did not nurture herself or the world enough in the painting of flowers which was, I believe, her true vocation, because it flowed from her like breath and gave equal happiness to herself and others. In giving ourselves to our true vocations we are creatures enjoying the natural ecstasy of being fully alive. This is so much better than aggravating ourselves into something that another person could do like life-giving breath, while we have to cough and sputter it out of us in breathless spasm. That is why I no longer try to paint! I am not my mother. I am myself.

For me, friendship is the finest art. Making connections with friends in mutual stimulation and exchange is truly life-giving, never life-sapping. If I feel life-sapped in a relationship, I know that I have been a sap by letting myself get into a one-way bond, and that is bondage. The giving and receiving do not have to be equal or always parallel, but may be delivered in subtle and staggered ways. Again, the whole pattern must be considered, and its duration over time. I may be doing all the giving during one phase of our relationship, and all the receiving during another. Or we may trust each other so completely that even the giver receives, though it is only the gift of unspoken appreciation or unuttered-but-felt satisfying love. Every friendship is a unique art form, an unmatchable bond, and its value can be measured only in terms of itself.

The friendship with the Creator which we call prayer is a model for all other friendships. Prayer is relationship. A relationship means being together, doing things together, experiencing things together, talking together, listening together, learning together, and feeling together. It is mutual self-revelation. Most of the time we show our love for each other simply by being together lovingly—and that is the essential form of prayer that comes with our merely being in the presence of God. But every relationship—including the one with our Creator—also requires that we take specific moments to tell each other, "I love you." Feeling beings such as ourselves—and our Creator—need to hear (and say) these words from time to time.

Sometimes relationship is silent communion. More often it is expressed—outered or uttered—communication. Communion is an energy field that fills and surrounds beings and makes all feel as one in the deepest sharing of felt experience. Communication is the direct linear flow from one going to another. It may be verbal, tactile, visual—it is usually sensual, but it may be nonphysical. It may be within the sensual realm of the imagination or the spirit—energy that transcends the body. That is how communication can defy distance.

I do not know if I learned this in intimate friendship with our Creator, or with human friends or other creatures, or simply all-one. But I know that this is how all relationship unfolds, and I am grateful to all my teachers—working, playing, praying together—for the blessed lesson.

I am particularly glad to know that even friendship is flawed and open for improvement. I need no deliberate Spirit Bead in any of my art, for I cultivate imperfection quite spontaneously. I make a good model for imperfection in all areas! That's reality.

Acceptance of reality is a key to happiness. I am finally learning this, too. It's never too late to catch on. I have a few theories of human development. The first is that we see the obvious last and forget it first. And so we need our friends to remind us of the obvious, as well as to love us despite our forgetfulness! That is why it takes so long for some of us to come to terms with reality and to be happy. The second is my porous onion theory.

As we grow, we gather new layers, and as we become well-rounded in our experience, the layers form in spiral circles. The layers are porous. At any moment it is likely that any layer may be stimulated to send its juices shooting up through the others to define the taste and smell of the surface—to make us weep or to sharpen the flavor of our lives. So we are like pungent or sweet onions, operating from many places and layers, all the times and ages of our lives. The hurt child of six may be in charge of a fifty-year-old's experience, or the happy child of ten lead the twenty- or eighty-year-old into unexplored feelings of delight. And that, given our complexity, is normal and apparently necessary, and so, it is all right. The trick is to be aware of it and to learn from it, taking the essence of the moment's interaction between the parts of ourselves and discovering how to direct or use what comes up.

Much of reality is painful, and learning to confront our past and present pain and incorporate it into the whole pattern is an essential way to add to the Great Harmony and our own happiness. Happiness is not blindness or blithering denial of the shadow-side of life, but the secret knowledge of how to bring it into harmony with the light, without shadow or light losing integrity, but each clarifying the other. I'm capable of being fundamentally happy in deep sorrow as in deep joy by trusting in the whole pattern. The onion is good—even if it momentarily makes me weep—and I trust the good of the whole to overcome the parts that are bad, avoiding in this way the bitter unhappiness that comes by letting one layer of it absorb me.

The reality of a particular moment may be horrible beyond bearing, truly evil in every way. There is no happy acceptance of it on any level. Yet that one moment is not ultimate. And what comes of it depends on the transforming power of the future, the will and desire to change. So a spoiled layer can be cut away or excised, even after it has been grown over, for its potency will prevail until it is fully seen and peeled, even from within. Remember, my onion is porous—it has some holes large enough to send down special instruments to explore and operate on inner levels of reality. But purity and joy depend on the recognition of what harms, as well as what helps and heals. Seeing is the beginning of healing. I may first only taste and smell what needs attending, but my instruments can help me to see and touch as well. The general becomes specific and something can be done. Then the power of the onion is manifold: It may send up stench and poison the air from a spoiled part below, or it may send up good flavor. Keep the onion sound and well, and it will be a source of intense pleasure by flavoring all experience, improving and adding interest to the varied dishes served up by life.

Out here in Oregon there is an onion that comes from Walla Walla, Washington, that is so sweet and mild, yet tangy, and it leaves no bad aftertaste or smell in the mouth. It must have taken generations to cultivate!

Only in recent years have I become aware of the potential for sweetness in the older layers of myself, those formed when I was young. When the older child was awakened in me, the younger child came out to play. Now I have access to all my ages, when before, a layer of gravity blocked my spiritual pores and I was only old. By the grace of God I found a good friend to help me open, so my innermost juices could flow to the surface with the wonder of play. Phil came into my life and invited me to come out and play in the open out-of-doors, perhaps for the first time. Phil—whose name means *friend*—loved my inner child out of her shyness. He married me and if I taught him to pray in new ways as he says I did, he taught me to play. He did this by the gift of joining together creatively and gracefully with me in deep friendship and sensuality, and by the gift of Pooh, Phil's first Christmas present to me.

Many Christmases later, Phil gave me a bear named Erasmus. That same year, I gave him a new twelve-string guitar called Alethea—Truth—in memory of his aunt Alice. He sold his old guitar—Erasmus—to my friend Jean for a gift for Luan. In exchange for that, and with what he was given for conducting a funeral, he gave me a new bear, named after music and after the *praise of folly* of Erasmus. He is a court jester bear and wears an elegant satin outfit, half royal blue and half old rose, with ivory lace collar and cuffs, and two silver bells on his pointed cap. Erasmus sits on a table in front of a crystal ball that rests on three golden unicorns. Under the table stands a large white unicorn named Firepearl. She has violet eyes and silver eyebrows and wears a wreath of flowers around her neck. Her legs are strong, and I imagine her luxurious white tail flowing in a black-sapphire sky as she flies into the night and a future time. Perhaps she carries Erasmus on her back, and together they glide between stars, creating an amethyst comet with a spiral path.

In the morning when I dress, I wonder what the future holds and how our lives will unfold. I breathe out my worry, for a dream messenger told me "Your job is not to worry, but to wait and write as you watch and work by the well." I look at Erasmus, smiling over his crystal ball. "Is it folly for me to be here, to have invested so much in an unknown future?"

The bear raises a velvet paw in blessing, and I sigh and blink and begin my day. After all, one is never too old for a happy childhood, just as it's never too late to grow up.

## Friends in Love

Friendship free and flowing,
Friendship tuned through time,
Friendship coming, going,
Friendship yours and mine.

Friendship caught on fire,
Friendship mountains deep,
Friendship souls' desire,
Friendship ours to keep.

*Eighteen*
# *In the Beginning . . .*

She is my Medicine Woman, one whom I can trust with my life and death. Mountain Shaman. Mandala Mountain. Sacred Triangle. Resting place for the eyes. Home of the soul. Giver of focus, and light.

It's spring. The purple crocus is gone. Lavender lilies are shooting up their first green stalks on the north side of the house. Emerald green velvet surrounds me. Daffodils are everywhere. The Mountain is molting—I now see bare rock where a month ago only white pads of snow showed on her shoulders. Earth Angel Mountain. Tonight the moon will again be full. And I am at the same time full and empty . . . *poured out like water*, as the psalmist said.

I came here hurt from demanding decisions from myself that I could not make; hurt from the weight of other people's needs; hurt from the ice of other people's fears and my own. In winter I broke through the fear barrier; later, the pain barrier. And then I began to learn again to release the hurt and heal myself anew. I held my eyes on the mandala of the Mountain and held my heart on the mantra of my prayer: "Into your hands I surrender my pain." Later, "Into your hands I commend us all for the good of all." In this time of arch-uncertainty in my life and the world's, all humankind seems congruent. It is the time to turn to the Holy One and wait upon Wisdom. Time to listen to the heartbeat of Mother Earth and synchronize our own with hers.

The shaman's work is to undergo mystical death and rebirth, to defend humanity against disease and destruction by transcending limits of the ego and learning from the larger life of the cosmos—through dying to self, abandoning ego-masks for a time. A common symbolic rite for this is to regard one's skeleton, to name and number one's bones, for bones are the essence of physical being and life. Blood is made in their marrow. Bones endure through millenia when the rest of the body has long returned to the body of earth. Through these longest-lasting parts of the body, the shaman is consecrated to life. This sacred rite is performed with the help of bears, and by the spirit of the moon.

The way to rebirth is in facing one's death.

Labor is difficult. The labor of birth hurts. It is hard work, harder than any other, for both mother and child. It is a dangerous work. We are not far from the days when it was common for either mother or child to die in the effort. Yet if one can survive the pain and the work, life follows to the full. Life will be faithful to those who have faithfully worked in the service of life. The labor to die is often the same as the labor to be born. The large life inside can no longer be contained. It struggles to break free, as the container struggles to break open. How hard to open, as well as to leave, the closed garden of the past, or of the body, in either birth or death. Delivery is accomplished only in the opening. My screams won't make it quicker. I have learned *that* in this time. I have learned to surrender to the process of becoming, to work with the rhythms of being. I am at least more comfortable in my inevitable discomfort. I have learned to be patient and rest between pushes. I am both mother and child.

These birth pangs are growing pains.

To learn of birth is to learn of death, and hardly know them from each other. Perhaps death, like the rest of life, and like birth, becomes what we make of it—as limited or unbounded as our choices make it. Or perhaps it is a surprise party. Or perhaps both. After all, life is a family project and my part in it is only a part.

This afternoon I put out oatbread crumbs for the Oregon juncos, little grey hopper-birds with black hoods. I watched them, fascinated, when suddenly a larger animal came into my view. It was a huge black and white dog—Princess, the Great Dane "puppy" from next door, accompanied by Sabrina the basset, smiling as ever. My neighbor Arty had told me that she worries when the two of them get out together for their doggy expeditions. Princess could elude a car on long Dane legs, but Sabrina's basset build and short legs could be her undoing. I tried to call Arty, but she was away on one of her trips—to work in Carmel or Vancouver, or visit her mother in Israel. I took the dogs home myself.

We ran through the meadow in the rain. Princess took off but Sabrina stayed right with me, delighted to have a playmate her own speed. I was surprised that my own body was small enough to crawl easily under my barbed wire fence. I said goodbye to the dogs, feeling much better for the exercise, and on the way back I laid my eyes on another animal new in the neighborhood: a jet black horse with a lightning white muzzle, named Shadow. He glows in the night and cuts the morning light with his body. How liberal of nature to play with black and white as much as with the broken light of rainbow prisms. In my dreams black and white are strong during times of life transition. Yin into Yang. The Tao dance continues.

The union of death and life was rhapsodized by Arty's young son Mark, who wrote this poem I saw one day in his mother's office: "A rainbow has colors/ it is curved like a skull/a rainbow is beautiful."

In mythic times the dog was sacred to the goddess, and guardian in the place of the dead. I ran easily with the dogs today. Above us the Angel Mountain glistened. I do not like to be too near the Mountain. One loses perspective. From here she is a great icon, inspiring, majestic, inviting me always to look up and ahead. She offers a goal, and a direction. I always know where I am in relationship to her. Those who climb the Mountain can lose this, and sometimes they lose themselves in the quest to conquer her or to dissolve their boundaries and become her. That is a dangerous violation.

Many have fallen into her crevasses and died. Others disappear at great heights and freeze to death. Those who climb cautiously are rewarded by an exhilarating perspective: they see other white mountains and the rolling body of the earth spread out before them in all directions for hundreds of miles. But they lose the proportions of the Mountain they're on, her body falsely foreshortened in their vertical vision. So misjudging their relationship to her, they can easily come to harm. For me, it is better below. I have been on top of other mountains looking across, and that was wonderful and good. But I do not want to break right relationship with my own Mountain by coming too close and falsifying my own position. From here, she is never a source of fear to me, but always of courage. My courage is not in conquest, but in companionship.

One night I dreamed I was in my grandmother's house at the foot of the Mountain. I went to lock the back door before sleep, and the keyhole was as big as my whole body! I felt like Alice looking through the Looking Glass out onto Wonderland—from my Grandma Alice's backdoor! Is the key to wonder through the body and its myriad miracles? How can we forget that to *sense* something is to know it instantly and deeply, or that *animal* derives from *anima*, which means *soul*? The way is unlocked from within, and the world of wonder awaits both beyond and within ourselves. Here lies the power which Alice Walker wrote of in the best sermon yet uttered, when her main character in *The Color Purple* said that it must hurt God when we walk by a field and don't even *see* the color purple, put there for sheer pleasure and delight. Joy is in the seeing, and seeing is in the being of the body, where spirit marries flesh to make soul.

In my recent dream, I am assisting a red-haired woman who faces a monumental task. She is to enter a sacred temple and speak with the dead. She prepares for the ceremony with dread, but then grows lighter as the time draws near. I open the great temple door and see an altar on which rests the dark head of an ancient philosopher. It is a head turned to stone from age—the Philosopher's Stone, the alchemical instrument of trans-formation. The spirit within is friendly and eager to pass on wisdom. The woman robed in white goes inside. I think that the neighborhood dogs could help her find her way back when she is finished. I send these black and white good beasts of the Goddess to guide her back, and all is well. All is as it is meant to be.

I am beginning to realize that somehow I came here to converse with the dead, to learn from those who have lived beyond what we know of life. I am still listening to them, still learning, and still delivering up what I have learned in the black and white of these pages.

There was thunder in the air under the Mountain today, and sharp cracks of lightning, yet the sun was shining brightly. I looked for liquid signs of the weather change, but that came much later. Weather seems incongruent here, but that may be because I still experience sequentially what to the larger earth and sky are polyphonous. It is a matter of perspective. The sound of the avalanche comes after the sight of it, because the speed of sound is slower than the speed of light, though they happen simultaneously. The eye and ear play at different speeds. We need to honor these natural distortions of perception before basing lasting judgments on them. Therefore, my constant warning to myself regarding my notions, myths, biases, assumptions, and opinions, whether personal or cultural and collective: Do not literalize your metaphors! I tell myself. They are most meaningful when malleable.

The coordination of all the powers of perception takes place over the whole pattern of a lifetime, so the conclusion can only be drawn when the pattern is completed. I believe that is true for the lifetimes of the universe, too. Such a great mystery unfolding from the hand of the Great Mystery, our loving Creator, in changeless change. . . .

Spring thunder is a sign of stirring life under the dead pruning piles. When the rains recede, they will take fire. Then the wildflowers can grow up from the ash and make way for summer.

We blessed beasts break the black earth under our feet as we run on her body, and breathe the white sky that rains to give us all life. Soon the black will give birth to bright green, and the rain will bring rainbow colors to bless the green with flowers, as the white heavens become blue with the new season. . . .

In the beautiful bliss of a country evening, sitting outside with Angel Mountain, clear at last in the twilight sky, only the sound of crickets, geese, and the River. Fresh grass smell, intoxicating. Spotlights on the Purple Splendor azalea and cotton candy rhododendron called Pink Pearl. The hundred white new balls on the

Snowball tree gleam in the shadowy dusk. The full moon is a fair pink peach, a disc resting on the horizon like a gigantic Host.

From my safe place at the foot of the Mountain I must compose what feeble comfort I can in a letter to Claire, whose son just died while climbing a mountain in the Alps, and who, not knowing I was actually here with my Mountain, sent word to me that she needed to hear about my love for mountains in order to help her comprehend her son's love and the meaning of his death.

Today I came home from a week in the Desert. A shimmering emerald frog no bigger than my thumb greeted me, sunbathing on the porch, its bronze eyelids sparkling over velvet black and red side markings. Over its head a bright green and black beetle shook its metallic wings. A welcome blessing. Life is so large and its mysteries so overwhelming. It is a comfort to come home to beauty. In this beauty is strength. In this beauty is trust. But in this beauty is no lulling against the storms. They come here, too.

I had tried to escape the possibility of storm by visiting friends in the Desert. But storms have a taste for the deserts of the south, so inviting in their open desolation. The high desert seems to beg for response from the sky. As in life, there is no place to hide from death, so the desert is no solace against the potential for desperation.

My friends in the Desert were loving and wise. Each offered counsel. Each blessed and comforted me in the confusion of my own journey. But their comfort was like that of Job's friends—it could not reach my innermost truth. For that, one friend took me to the top of a desert mountain overlooking other mountains and a few valiant lakes. Below us, utter desolation; around us, a mercilessly hot wind; and above us, a human butterfly gliding with red wings, and free.

I sat in the shade of a great rock with my old friend silently beside me, and I began to face the deepest reality which my Oregon meadows and forest held in promise, yet kept me from moving decisively toward in their distracting sensuality. Like Job, but for different reasons, I had sat in one place delayed and dismayed, not knowing how to move into the future, unable to heed the reasonable advice of others. Then on an ancient dinosaur dungheap overlooking a desert, complete with tormenting red ants, where beauty and wretchedness mingle indistinguishably, I opened my eyes. There in the desert wasteland of what I called Job's Mountain, I saw starkly my alternatives: fly free or die of thirst. Still, I could not overcome my idea that freedom also meant death, and so I had been frozen. . . . But perhaps the whole matter was out of my hands, and there was no decision at all for me to make. I simply had to wait. I said aloud the German poet Rilke's words in English: "The most painful decision is not as bad as the anguished cry, 'What shall I do?' " Though I released myself from the obligation to act, I was also able to let go of that cry by which I had lived for nearly two years.

Now, it seems, is the time for patience and trust, and nothing more. Alas! And Thank God.

My silent companion then spoke:

"You must be trusting of yourself now. You must be true to your innermost feelings. Have faith in the future. God is with you to shield you and strengthen you. Life will sustain you. You are loved." These words somehow echoed and amplified the words of blessing with which I had begun my journey in Minnesota months earlier.

I felt that I had been stuck in the middle of a bridge for a very long time, unable to move forward fearing the possibility of nothing on the other side, and yet unwilling to go back. My friend reminded me of the obvious: one foot in front of the other! Later we went to a new bridge crossing the Salmon River back in Oregon. I had found the bridge in Wildwood my first spring back here and had crossed it only that first time. As we walked along a muddy trail for a few hundred yards, I realized that in all the times I'd returned to show the bridge to my houseguests, I never went beyond the middle of it. This time, I went onto the bridge alone, stood in the middle, and looked back where I'd come from to see a paved sunlit path and bright, friendly trees, all familiar. I looked down into the shadows on the other side and saw—nothing. How could I get myself over there? One foot in front of the other. I visualized people I loved on the known path above me saying, "We love you. You can do it. Go on." Then I visualized loving faces on the other side, beckoning to me. I began, watching my feet and the new wooden beams under them. Soon I realized my feet were no longer on wooden beams, but sunlit pavement. I looked up to find that I had been off the bridge for some time, not even noticing the moment of actual transition. To my surprise, the muddy path had been beautifully paved since that first time, and the way was secure beneath my feet, the trees as bright and welcoming as those on the other side. I laughed. Now to carry the triumph into my everyday life. One foot in front of the other.

Back in the desert, we drove down the mountain from Job's Rock to the desert floor, and that night my friend taught me to trust the black water of a swimming pool under the night sky, encouraging me to let myself go under with the confidence that I could come up again when I chose to. Again and again I submerged myself and held my breath, until I believed that I would not die. I changed my focus from the fear of water overwhelming and drowning me to confidence in its power to hold me up so that I could move myself through it and be supported. The message was not lost on me. The lesson on Job's Mountain and the lesson in the dark pool were the same. Within minutes that night, I was teaching myself to swim—my same old head-above-water bear crawl, but with a new ease and grace, for I was unafraid for the first time. It was not water that I had feared, but suffocation. I didn't move in the direction of my desire because I feared that if I once held my breath or lost it, I would never get it back. I was wrong.

Now I've come back once again to my Mountain. Each day, all through the day, and every night in my dreams, I practice swimming. I revise and revive my belief in myself and in the future, and in the presence of God abiding and sustaining me. I consecrate everything,

everything, including my old fear and disbelief, as material for deep transformation, and I allow trust to re-create in me and the gift of faith to flow through me. I remember a friend's question in the Desert: "What part of your life is the center of everything else? As a professional woman, do you trace your creativity to poetry or priesthood or therapy or teaching or writing?"

"The creative life is the consecrated life," I answered. "For me, priesthood as consecration is definitive. All healing and creativity spring from that center. Consecrated living is living with eyes open, with recognition; and with heart open, with receptivity and outpouring gratitude. Poet and performer are one, healer and teacher are one, and all these to me are priestly because they show and celebrate reality at the deepest point of relationship. I know I was born to be both celebrant and lover."

I asked my inner Angel, "What is crucial?" And the answer was, "Readiness." It can take a long time. It requires steadfast practice, like the habit of happiness. I am finally swimming. I am finally ready.

I have dared to speak from the heart of my own transition, from the middle of my bridge, trusting that the voice in the wilderness is a valid voice, that I need not keep silent until I reach the promised land. The way itself is a blessing.

In a few moments it will be midnight and the first Sunday of spring. I bless the earth and myself and pray over all our seasons, "Let it unfold." I trust the times and open myself to the light that waits in the dark. I feel blessed, as the sweet confusion of nature is blessed in transition—bright buds breaking through rotting leaves. I catch my breath and push again, then rest, and look to the Mountain for courage.

She is my Mother. She is my Midwife.

## *AND*

*I heard a voice from heaven . . .
saying to me, "Write."*
The Book of Revelation

*In my end is my beginning. . . .*
Last words of Mary, Queen of Scots

O God, thou has searched me out, and known me.
Thou knowest my down-sitting and mine up-rising;
thou understandest my thoughts long before.

Thou art about my path, and about my bed;
and art acquainted with all my ways.

For lo, there is not a word in my tongue,
but thou, O God, knowest it altogether.

Thou has beset me behind and before,
and laid thine hand upon me.

Such knowledge is too wonderful and excellent for me;
I cannot attain unto it.

Whither shall I go then from thy Spirit?
Or whither shall I go then from thy presence?

If I climb up into heaven, thou art there;
if I go down to hell, thou art there also.

If I take the wings of the morning,
and remain in the uttermost parts of the sea;

Even there also shall thy hand lead me,
and thy right hand shall hold me.

If I say Peradventure the darkness shall cover me;
then shall my night be turned to day.

Yea, the darkness is no darkness with thee,
but the night is as clear as the day;
the darkness and light to thee are both alike.

For my reins are thine;
thou hast covered me in my mother's womb.

I will give thanks unto thee, for I am
fearfully and wonderfully made: marvellous are thy works,
and that my soul knoweth right well

My bones are not hid from thee,
though I be made secretly, and fashioned
beneath in the earth.

Thine eyes did see my substance, yet being imperfect;
and in thy book were all my members written;

Which day by day were fashioned,
when as yet there was none of them.

How dear are thy counsels unto me, O God;
O how great is the sum of them!

If I tell them, they are more in number
than the sand; when I wake up,
I am present with thee. . . .

        from Psalm 139
        adapted from the King James Version

# About the Author

Alla Renée Bozarth is the daughter of an artistic Russian immigrant mother and an Episcopal priest father. Her mother painted. Her father wrote poetry. Both were dramatic performers.

As an only child, Alla absorbed the artistic and spiritual gifts of her parents as her legacy.

She traces her vocation as a spiritual midwife symbolically to her great-grandmother, a teacher and midwife, and to her mother, who worked through Church World Service to help displaced persons find new homes. Her passion for the sensual and meaningful word comes from her paternal grandmother, with whom much of her childhood was spent in the shared enjoyment of literature—from Shakespeare and the Psalms to Allen Ginsberg and Emily Dickinson. Alla also draws inspiration from her Osage Indian great-great-grandmother, who was a self-taught linguist.

During her academic years in theology and the performing arts at Northwestern University, Alla received an urban education, marching to Peoria in the Hunger Caravan with Jesse Jackson and experiencing the powerful emotions of the peace and justice movements of the early seventies.

Later she married her seminary colleague and moved from Chicago to Minneapolis, where she developed Wisdom House—a healing and worshiping community. Alla's marriage of fourteen years was creatively rich, as she shared dance and music in ministry with her Episcopal priest husband, a profoundly gifted singer. After his sudden death in 1985, Alla returned to her earth-roots at the foot of Mt. Hood in western Oregon, where her priestly ministry continues and she experiences healing and growth "through the mystery of being alone—all one" in the presence of her "personal power spots—the sacred Mountain and the gypsy Ocean" of the Oregon Coast.